# GOD, MY POTTER AND I, HIS CLAY

# GOD, MY POTTER AND I, HIS CLAY

PL Yip

PARTRIDGE
A Penguin Random House Company

Print information available on the last page.

**To order additional copies of this book, contact**
Toll Free 800 101 2657 (Singapore)
Toll Free 1 800 81 7340 (Malaysia)
orders.singapore@partridgepublishing.com

www.partridgepublishing.com/singapore

# Contents

# Introduction

**\*\*\*\*\*\*\*\*\*\***

"Gong Gong, can you tell me something about your early childhood?" Melissa, my ten-year old grand-daughter asked me inquisitively one day. Earlier on, when the family was discussing dental hygiene among us, I casually remarked to Sook Cheng, my elder daughter, "Do you know I could have been your dentist? I was offered admission to study dentistry by the King Edward VII College of Medicine, Singapore, after completing my Cambridge School Certificate Examination. I just did not have the money then and I failed to get a scholarship. So my dream of becoming a dentist, like so many of my dreams, remains just a dream." Oh, was she surprised! "Huh! Really Pa? This is the first time after forty years that I heard about this!" Sook Cheng said unbelievingly. "Yes, there are many more things you children don't know about me," I added. "Pa, you should write a book about yourself for posterity and for the family to get to know you better," suggested William, my son-in-law. But I said to myself I am not a high-profiled individual and have achieved nothing reputable in society. I am just an ordinary, spry senior Malaysian citizen enjoying my pension. Pondering over it for a while, I agreed it was not a bad idea after all to leave something about myself for my family to read. To kick-start such a big project,

I thought it would be best to write my life chronicles by tracing them through the various home addresses which I had stayed previously.

It took me quite a while to choose an appropriate title for my book to match some of my life experiences of ups and downs as well as failures and successes. Finally, by the grace of God, I picked this title: "God, My Potter and I, His Clay – some highlights of my life experiences as a Christian believer", as I endeavour to illustrate how God, my Heavenly Father shaped and moulded me as a potter would his clay, from a helpless seven-year old orphan to what He wanted me to become – a successful professional social worker. In between, I had encountered toils and snares, but each time I came out unscathed.

So, put on your life jackets, sit back and relax. I take you on a cruise of twists and turns down the choppy and meandering waters of my chronicles, as I unfold to you some of my more interesting milestones to give you some insight of who I am.

*PL Yip*

*I dedicate this book to my beloved
wife, Swee Yeng, my three filial children,
Sook Cheng, Sook Leng and Ming Fai
as well as their caring spouses, William Chew,
Austin Chan and Sandie Toh. And last but
not least, to my three precious grandchildren,
Aaron, Joelle and Melissa.*

*Yip Peng Low*

# About The Author

Born on 13 April, 1928 to a Malayan Railway Clerk father and illiterate housewife mother, I became a nobody's child at the tender age of 7, when both my parents succumbed to tuberculosis. Second among six siblings, we were brought up separately by our paternal aunts. I was fortunate to stay with my Sam Ku Cheh (third paternal aunt) and her police clerk husband together with their children, soon after I became an orphan.

From primary school, owing to poverty, I was exempted from paying school fees, right up to my final year in the elite Penang Free School. Later on, at the age of 26, I was privileged to continue to enjoy free education to pursue the Diploma in Social Studies at the University of Malaya at the Bukit Timah campus in Singapore, when I was awarded a federal government scholarship. Thus, it can be said, I was one of the lucky ones to be exempted from tuition fees throughout my entire education from Primary 2.

If resumes were in vogue for job applications in the 1950s, then my list of work experiences would read, *Yiu-Chah-Kueh* hawker, *nonya* cake seller, newspaper vendor, apprentice refrigerator mechanic, private tutor, English school trainee teacher and Japanese college lecturer would have appeared in my application for the post of social worker.

An English lady, my primary school headmistress, expressed her desire to adopt me while I was in my early days of bereavement. But the blessed One who created me was to come into my life in later years to adopt me as His child. He made me the kind of person He wanted me to be, moulding and shaping me all along as a Potter would, his clay. For 33 years, I served as a social welfare officer with the Ministry of Welfare Services in Malaysia.

Little did I imagine a poor orphan like me would one day be given privileged leave to tour Europe with my wife on a government grant. Neither did I dream, this twelve-year-old street hawker would one day report at the Office of the United Nations Development Programme inside the majestic United Nations Building in New York on a UN fellowship grant; nor did I fancy that even during my retirement and already in my early sixties, my wife and I were able to travel to Cambridge University to attend Ming Fai's graduation.

Have you experienced enemy air raids over your heads? Well, I had. I was living in the police barracks when Japanese planes dropped bombs on the police headquarters on 10th December 1941, at the beginning of World War II. By God's grace, I was snatched from the jaws of death.

I used to worship the Lord at the Island Glades Gospel Centre at Yeap Chor Ee Road in Penang during my early retirement, but I am presently attending Bethesda Serangoon Church at Upper Serangoon Road in Singapore since 1997.

God, by His tender mercies, has granted me a devoted wife. By his grace, He has blessed me with three obedient and filial children, two daughters and a son. Under His guidance, I have fulfilled my obligations as a parent to raise them up happily, finance their tertiary education adequately and finally, marry them off joyfully. Now, in my twilight years, just about to reach 80, God willing, I am enjoying each day, the comforts and new mercies of God, remembering that each day is a bonus from Him.

So, do you see the wonderful but unseen hand of God, shaping and holding me up? As a born-again Christian, I certainly do as I continue to share with you other testimonies of my experiences with God in this book.

# Prologue

The memoir of our beloved father entitled "God, My Potter and I, His Clay" is truly by far Pa's greatest accomplishment. As I typed his manuscripts prior to his demise and shortly after he was called home to the Lord, these chronicles gave me a greater insight into the man that my father was.

From a tender age of seven, he was already an orphan, shunted from one home to another. Without any proper parental guidance, yet this remarkable man accomplished so much in his life time. He went on to make something of himself, touched many lives and even right till the time of his death, he was still thinking of others. One cannot help but wonder how he could be such a loving husband, a terrific father when he did not really have a role model to follow. His love for the family was unconditional.

Pa embarked on this memoir in 2007 but sadly he did not complete the final chapter of this book. The task fell upon our brother, Ming Fai, to finish the race for him. I thank God that William, my brother-in-law, managed to encourage Pa to write his memoir, even though I had urged him to do so some years back as I listened enthralled by his many interesting stories.

He took great comfort in God's Word and drew closer to God as his body was ravaged by his ailment. Pa's walk with God was indeed an inspiration to all of us who knew him. He had a generous heart, a wonderful sense of humour, and was fastidious and meticulous with all that he was entrusted with. As a result of his personal relationship with God, we as his children walk in his blessings. He never failed to encourage us, taking pride in all our accomplishments no matter how trivial they may be. What a terrific role model to emulate.

As his story unfolds, one cannot help but admire this remarkable man for his excellent memory and his ability to recall names of his childhood friends. In his final months, he was writing feverishly as if he knew that he was slowly coming to an end of the chapter of his life on earth.

May he be an inspiration to you as he was to his family.

*Sook Leng*

# 25 Ceylon Lane
# Circa: 1930-1934

I was born on 13 April 1928, year of the Dragon, according to the Chinese calendar, at One Kuala Kangsar Road in Penang, second among six children. I remember very little of my infancy and toddlerhood here. However, I can recall some of my early childhood experiences during my stay at 25 Ceylon Lane. It is appropriate for me to begin my chronicles from this house. First, let me introduce you to my father, Yip Kum Seng. He was tall and was of medium built, until he fell very ill. He was English educated and worked as a railway clerk at godown No. 5 Weld Quay, Penang. He was a generous person, showering us and my cousins living nearby with toys and gifts on festive occasions like Chinese New Year. There was one occasion when he gave each of us a box of multi- coloured glass marbles and I had a happy time playing them with my siblings and cousins. My father also enjoyed playing with fire crackers to celebrate the ninth night of the Chinese New Year with a big bang. I would sit at a safe distance, covering my ears to keep away the loud din, as I watched the thrilling and exciting annual spectacle.

One day, when I arrived home from school, I was rushed upstairs to see my father. I wondered why, as I climbed up the stairs. I was shocked to see him lying in bed with a heavily bandaged right hand – the result of his brave intervention in a fight between some coolies with sickles in the godown.

I started school at Wellesley Primary School, a government school, when I was six years old. It was within walking distance from my house and my first aunt, whom I called Ku-Ma, brought me lunch in a tiffin-carrier during school recess.

Now, here is my fondest memory of my father. Even at this moment, I still remember very vividly this happy time with him. One day, just before the annual school holidays, after my Primary 1 examination, he called me, putting me on his lap, while lying on his deck chair. He held the local newspaper, "The Straits Echo" in front of me. He directed me with his finger to read the news. To my surprise, I discovered that the newspaper had published the names of all the prize winners of my school. My name was there as the first prize winner in Primary 1! That was the first time my name appeared in the media. I was so happy and my father was so proud of me. Hugging me and ruffling my hair, he urged me to continue studying hard so that I could be among the top students every year. So endearing was that brief moment to both of us, that I would often replay the image in my thoughts, and it has etched on my mind ever since. But alas, that was to be his last hug for me even though I topped the class in subsequent years, for I lost him the following year to tuberculosis.

# 71D Kedah Road
# Circa 1935-1940

This was to be my house of double tragedy, for at the age of seven, within a short space of six months, I lost both my parents who succumbed to tuberculosis when I was in Primary 2. My father must have contracted this disease when I was in Primary 1, and subsequently infected my mother. I remembered visiting my father in the General Hospital and watching people play polo on horseback at the polo ground opposite his ward window. There was a brief period when I was put to stay with my Sam Ku Cheh at 28 Ceylon Lane, just opposite my previous house, while my parents left for Brastagi, a health resort in Sumatra for TB patients, for further treatment. But alas, he did not find a cure and his condition deteriorated.

He then returned to Penang without any hope to survive. He was 39 years old as he lay on his deathbed in the second hall downstairs. I still recall very vividly his very last moment on his deathbed. That particular morning while I was playing with my siblings in the main hall, I suddenly heard screams followed by loud wailings from my mother and aunts coming from the second hall. "Ah Seng! Ah Seng! Don't go yet. Open your eyes!" they shouted "Children, come here quickly!" my mother yelled. We rushed in hurriedly. I saw my father, very weak and frail, sitting up and leaning against the wall, gesturing with both hands for a change of clothes. "Quick! Kneel down and kow-tow to your father. Call Papa! Call Papa!" someone shouted. My father knew he was slipping away and wanted to put on his special funeral clothes before he was to be put into the coffin afterwards. These special clothes had been bought in advance for such an eventuality.

Now, let me highlight a couple of funeral rites practised at that time. As the eldest son, my brother Peng Lum, had to put on all the seven layers of the funeral clothes assisted by the undertaker, and then these clothes were to be transferred on to my father later on. My brother had to stand on a low stool on the five-foot way with outstretched arms sideways to put on layer after layer of the clothes, each of a different colour. After all the seven layers of funeral clothes were piled onto my brother, the undertaker then removed all these clothes at one go, and put those on the limp body of my father. He also put on a black cloth cap and black shoes to complete the full attire before placing my father on a wooden make-shift bed in the main hall. Next, the Taoist priest chose an auspicious hour to lead the six of us down the road to perform a ritual known as "*mai sui*" (in Cantonese, meaning to buy water), where a basin of water had earlier been put in place at a spot on the road to be "bought" by my brother who used it to wash my father's face and body under the supervision of the priest. Later, in the afternoon, my uncle took both of us to purchase the coffin. After my uncle had carefully selected one, both my brother and I were asked to write our names on one of the wooden corners of the coffin for easy identification when delivered to the house later.

It was one of the mores among Cantonese mourners to wail and cry in a special way, as they knelt before the dead, whenever the Taoist priest conducted his prayer rituals. Such special mourners had a knack of mourning over the dead, quite different from the ordinary mourners, who would just sob and sniff and sway their heads in deep bereavement. My first paternal aunt, Ku-Mah was such a special mourner. As she cried with a handkerchief, she would sing loud appeals to my father in short, melancholic refrains, with high and low pitches: something like this:

"Ah Seng! Oh, Ah Seng,

You must bless all of us, especially your six small children wherever you are.

They are so very pitiful, as you leave them.

No one will feed them. Why do you go away so early, Oh Ah Seng?

We are very sorrowful, have pity on us, Ah Seng!"

When Cantonese families did not have such a mourner among the family members, they would pay the undertaker to acquire for them a professional mourner for a fee. But such a custom is no longer the fashion among the modern Cantonese.

While it must have been very painful for my father to leave the six of us behind whose ages ranged between 2 - 11 years, the more so for my young, widowed mother in her mid-thirties to feed us. She was just an ordinary housewife, uneducated and was often bullied by my maternal uncle and second paternal aunt whenever these people had arguments with my mother.

Soon after the funeral was over, the adults began discussing among themselves very seriously how to bring us up. My mother was already impoverished by my parents' protracted illness. My Ku Ma, aged 40-odd was an unemployed spinster, while my 2nd paternal aunt's husband was a labourer in a tin-smelting company and had two children. Only Sam Ku Cheh, my third and youngest paternal aunt, in her mid thirties, was better off than her elder sisters. Her husband was a clerk in the police department and she had two children too. Someone suggested that the six of us be sent to the Convent orphanage so that we could be together. Ku Ma objected strongly lest we be converted to Catholics. Eventually, a compromise was reached among the adults, whereby second aunt would adopt my youngest sister, Moon Yeng, aged 2. Sam Ku Cheh agreed to look after me as I had established much earlier a close rapport with my cousins in my previous sleepovers.

The rest of my siblings – Peng Lum, aged 11, Moon Toh, aged 6, and twins Peng Yew and Moon Yoke, aged 4, remained with my mother and my Ku Ma. It must have been very difficult for my mother to raise the money to feed my four siblings. She must have literally begged from her elder brother who was a local dentist by profession and also an opium addict, for financial support occasionally. Each time he would raise his voice at my mother, belittling and scolding her to show that she was not welcomed.

On one occasion, when my mother took me with her, I was very angry with my uncle for shouting and scolding my mother with gestures and verbal abuse, that I told her not to approach him in future. But she replied very gently and said, "You are still young; you don't understand things yet." As I reminisce now, I can appreciate her hardships and sufferings; she had endured herself to support us as well as to find the money for her medical treatment. Her sacrifices must had taken a heavy toll on her health for some six or seven months after my father's death, she too, left us when she was just 35 years old.

When she died, I was the only child not by her bedside. A cousin, the daughter of my second paternal aunt, had rushed over to inform me of my mother's imminent death. I ran as fast as I could to Kedah Road, dreading I might not see her alive for the last time. A sense of foreboding crept in my mind, and grief overcame me when I saw my mother already dressed in funeral clothes, lying on the makeshift wooden bed, when I reached home. My Ku Ma called loudly to my mother, "Peng Low has come home already. You can now leave us peacefully." I was coaxed to look at my mother for the last time, before her entire face was covered with some joss papers, "Kneel and kow tow to your mother," someone said to me. I sobbed loudly as I joined my siblings to kneel before my mother as a symbol of our filial piety. Once more, we wore black attire all over again and began our months of bereavement for my mother.

# 35 Ariffin Road
# Circa 1935-1940

This was where I lived with Sam Ku Cheh and her family from 7 to 12 years old. But the condition of the house was certainly not in ruins then, contrary to the photograph below, as this was taken around 2006.

One of my saddest chronicles of my past history took place here, soon after my mother's death. One day, Sam Ku Cheh beckoned me to stand in front of her. I wondered why. Wagging her finger at me, she warned, "Don't you ever dare to be naughty. You don't have your father and mother to protect you now. Do you understand?" I was shocked at her sudden outburst. I had not misbehaved myself recently and so failed to understand her reprimand. Among my three paternal aunts, I adored her most. She was the one whom I had the most respect, for she was always by nature, a kind, sympathetic and generous person. I was indeed surprised by her warning. I was already sad, having lost both my parents whom I loved very much. I certainly did not want to be reminded about this tragedy. Her sharp words tore into my heart and brought me tears. I dared not sob in her presence, lest she might accuse me of bringing misfortune to her, should she encounter ill luck. I quickly dashed into the bathroom and began to splash buckets of water on my face, ostensibly to bathe, but actually, it was to drown my sobs for my dead parents. I had many fond memories of my parents whom I adored very much. Many a night, as I slept with my cousins, I would silently cry myself to sleep, letting my tears trickle down my face to be soaked up by the corners of my soft pillow, as I pined for them.

The double deaths of my parents soon caught the attention of my school head mistress, Miss R. Duncan, an English lady and also my music teacher, Miss Hong Yeng. Both felt very sorry for me and had expressed their keenness to adopt me, to give me a new home and to see to my education. But my aunts were not in favour of their adoption but pleaded with the principal for financial assistance, so that I could continue my education. Soon afterwards, our appeal for school aid was approved and from Primary 2 that year, I became a free scholar up to university, in the sense that I was exempted from paying tuition fees. I studied diligently in response to the government's sponsorship for my education at Wellesley Primary School (up to Standard 1), Hutchings School (Standard 2 to Standard 5) and eventually at the elite Penang Free School from Standard 6, until war broke out, when Japan occupied Malaya after driving out the British forces. I topped my class in all my examinations every term without any private tuition.

When I was the top student again in the first term in Standard 3 at Hutchings School, I was promoted to Standard 4 the following term. In other words, I was given a double promotion in one year. While

I felt jubilant, it was a big struggle for me initially to cope with this accelerated promotion, and there were no remedial classes to help me along. Yet, I did not fare too badly in the two subsequent term tests, ranking 5th and 3rd respectively. I had always been very industrious in my studies and need not be reminded to do my homework. Occasionally, I sought help though in mathematics from my cousin, Ming, who was two levels ahead of me. However, in the following year, Standard 5, I reclaimed my top position again. Elated though I was, I felt sad at the same time because my father was not around to share my joy and success. The only reward I got was a piece of roast duck drumstick from my Ku Ma, my first paternal aunt. In spite of her poverty, she would still scrimp to find the money to reward me ungrudgingly.

It was while staying in this house that I became exposed to the Cantonese opera through my cousin, Yong, who was 2 years my senior. She showed a very keen interest in this performing art. Actually, her father was given a complimentary pass for two adults to watch the show, but she could not find an equally enthusiastic companion for the opera and so she picked me. We would usually hitch a rickshaw ride to watch the opera in the amusement park almost every weekend night. I became an opera buff in no time.

Now, there was a time when I observed that my uncle began to drive a car, upgrading himself from a motorcycle. It was a brand new MG sports car and I would sometimes be taken out for evening car rides with the family. The seats smelling of new leather, were so comfortable and the engine had a soft purring sound. He must be quite a rich man, I thought to myself. As if to confirm my thoughts, I saw some afternoons later, a jeweller in the house working painstakingly to design and set pieces of jewellery, like ear-rings and necklace, in sparkling diamonds for my aunt. Indeed he must be wealthy now to afford such expensive jewelleries. Or in fact, was he really?

The sports car and the precious diamonds were gifts presented to my uncle and aunt by a young, wealthy widow, who had befriended my uncle. These gifts were in fact bribes, offered to my aunt with a hope that she would accept the widow as my uncle's mistress. In accepting these costly gifts, my aunt had thus condescended to acknowledge this lady officially as a member of the family. So, an auspicious day was chosen for this lady to move in. I believed a simple tea ceremony, as is the custom, must have taken place, whereby the young mistress had to offer tea to my aunt, and address my aunt as "elder sister." In ancient days in China, the wife would then give a new name to the concubine or mistress, but in this instance, my aunt opted to abstain. Luk Ku (meaning 6th aunt, as she was probably the 6th child in her family) was how we addressed her. She moved in together with her two small daughters from her previous marriage to occupy the front bedroom (just vacated by a married couple tenant), while Sam Ku Cheh and her two children and I remained in the second room.

During the early days of living together under the same roof, both Sam Ku Cheh and Luk Ku showed mutual respect for each other, exchanging pleasantries now and then, and speaking kindly to each other. My uncle was quite diplomatic and was able to share his time adequately between his two wives to make the two of them happy but for a while only. This was the lull to the impending storm.

As time went by, jealousy between the wives began to rear its ugly head. Both women began to find fault with each other, petty though they might be. Frequent marital spats exploded among the trio, even spilling into the middle of the night, when we were all asleep, putting pressure on my poor uncle to pacify his wives. It must have been very distressing for him, not only losing his precious sleep, but his violent temper as well, as he shouted and raged at his wives whose bedrooms were separated by a thin wooden partition. The women would not be intimidated easily by his temper tantrums, laced with coarse language and expletives unprintable here. They continued with their heated exchanges unabated, so much so, that my uncle would bang the wooden wall with his fists. He even resorted to pummeling his bare chest, trying to quieten them. You can imagine the loud din in the middle of the night, caused by my uncle's shouting and his banging the walls in the course of these quarrels. There was one such occasion, when I could not help eavesdropping on my uncle threatening to shoot himself dead to appease his wives. Suddenly, there was some commotion in our bedroom as Sam Ku Cheh tried to snatch the gun from my uncle, who was licensed to carry a gun. My cousins and I cowered with fear and we quickly covered our bodies from head to toe with our blankets, expecting the worse. But fortunately, nothing untoward came out of this threat, as calm prevailed eventually to save the situation.

"Good news, everybody!" my uncle shouted as he returned from work one day. Smiling happily, he continued, "I've been allotted quarters. We are going to stay in the barracks of the new police headquarters. So get ready to move house any time now!" he added.

The Penang Police Headquarters, facing the Chowrasta market, is a magnificent five-storey grey, concrete square building bounded by Penang Road, Khoo Sian Ewe Road, Transfer Road and Dickens Road. While the police administrative departments were mainly housed in the blocks facing Penang Road and Dickens Road, the police personnel and civilian staff were quartered at barracks along the blocks facing Khoo Sian Ewe Road and Transfer Road. There is a large square quadrangle within the four concrete blocks for police drills and occasional parades.

My uncle who worked as the chief clerk was allotted a 3-bedroom unit at the ground floor facing Transfer Road with modern sanitation. I liked the toilet which came fitted with a flush system, and with just one pull of the lever, everything was gone. It was unlike the bucket system we were so used to in our previous homes, where we discharged our faeces through a small round hole inside the toilet into a rubber bucket, which the sewage labourer would replace usually in the early hours of the morning with a clean one, through an opening outside the toilet wall, with his bare hands. He would then carry the dirty and smelly bucket filled with faeces to empty it into a waiting sewage truck along the back lanes.

Parents used to warn their children they would become sewage coolies if they were lazy and did not study hard, alluding that to be the lowest occupation one should try to avoid. There was adequate accommodation for the whole family. Sam Ku Cheh and her husband occupied the front room; my two cousins took the second room while the domestic servant and I shared the third, all of which were very spacious. Luk Ku and her two daughters had moved out to stay on their own. My life was a bed of roses here, receiving my daily pocket money, having my clothes washed and I had the privilege of going to school by car. But my two school going brothers staying at Amoy Lane with Ku Ma (first paternal aunt) were less fortunate. I was in Standard 6 attending the premier Penang Free School while my cousin was in Standard 8, and his sister was in Standard 7 of another reputable girls' school, the St. George's Girls School. I enjoyed my school days very much and could cope very well with my studies. I even took up Latin in school which was a pre-requisite for students aspiring to study legal studies. I continued to excel in my examination and was awarded with two prizes, General Merit and Science.

Sam Ku Cheh was as usual kind and loving towards me and easily approachable. She would almost daily frequent the mahjong sessions organised by Ku Ma at Amoy Lane, not so much as to gamble, but primarily to support Ku Mah's idea to tax the mahjong players in order to feed my siblings under her care. The more hours the players indulge in the mahjong session, the more money Ku Mah would collect.

As I had been spending most of my days with my two cousins, I rarely interacted with my own siblings. I would occasionally bump into them when I accompanied my female cousin to visit her mother at the mahjong sessions in Amoy Lane. Contacts with them, if any, were brief and few and far between. Thus, in a way, I was more attached to my cousins and rather detached from my siblings, and so relationship with the latter seems cursory.

Sometime around November, there had been rife speculations by the majority of the population that Japan would inevitably ally with Germany and Italy, the so-called Axis Power to attack Britain and America, the Allied Forces. Germany and Italy were already at war with England and the rest of Europe with America actively providing arms and other essential war supplies to England. Malaya was under British rule and in anticipation of a Japanese invasion; the civilian population was given emergency drills like air raid exercises. Many were to join voluntary organisations like the LDC (Local Defence Corp) and ARP (Air Raid Precaution), set up to beef up the civil defences of the country. My uncle was a volunteer with the ARP and I remembered him putting on his steel helmet with the inscription of ARP on the front of it whenever he volunteered for air raid duty. Whenever enemy planes were sighted, air raid sirens would be sounded and the people advised to run for cover in air raid shelters or in their homes until a continuous and monotonous wail would signal the end of the raid.

On 8th December, 1941, Japan officially declared war on America and Britain. This signalled the beginning of World War II. (Note: World War II actually started on 1st September 1939 when Germany invaded Poland). On 9th December, 1941, the Japanese armed forces with lightning speed surprised the British by capturing Kota Bahru, capital of the State of Kelantan in Malaya. On the same day, on the mainland opposite Penang Island, the British military airport in Butterworth came under swift attack by the Japanese. For a while, at least in the early days of the Malayan campaign, the Japanese air force proved so formidable that two British navy battleships, HMS The Prince of Wales and HMS Repulse, the pride of the British navy were sent to their watery graves together with their crew, just because the battleships simply had no air cover.

By 15 February, 1942, Malaya including Singapore finally capitulated to the Japanese Imperial Army led by Lt. Gen Yamashita, who after the war ended was charged for war atrocities by the Allied Forces and executed.

Now let me highlight a very interesting but scary experience associated with this war. I was thirteen years old then, with my annual school vacation interrupted by the Japanese invasion. My first and most frightening encounter with this war came about on the 9th December 1941. Around 9.00 am, air raid sirens announced the approach of Japanese war planes. We locked our doors and soon we heard drones of enemy planes faintly at first but grew louder as they flew over the Police headquarters. Instinctively, Sam Ku Cheh pulled the three of us and our domestic servant quickly under her large master bed. We were advised to prop up cotton mattresses all around the four legs of the bedstead to protect us from machine gun bullets. Hardly had we settled down comfortably under the bed, when I heard several very loud explosions from bombs and rapid machine gun fire for the first time in my life. The administrative block of the Police Headquarters was being bombed and we heard machine gun fire sprayed by the speedy planes unchallenged, as they zoomed low to unleash their bombs on their targets. There seemed to be no resistance from the British anti-aircraft batteries nor from their Spitfires and Hurricanes to challenge them.

My aunt was clutching to Kuan Yin, the goddess of mercy to keep us safe. Then came this sudden thunderous and deafening explosion, so close to our living quarters, sending all of us clutching one another, screaming and crying as if our quarters had been hit. I wondered in silence, "Will the building collapse on us?"

*But now thus says the Lord who created you, O Jacob, and He who formed you, O Israel: "Fear not, for I have redeemed you; I have called you by your name; you are Mine. When you pass through the waters, I will be with you; and through the rivers, they shall not overflow you. When you walk through the fire, you shall not be burned; nor will the flame scorch you. For I am the Lord your God, the Holy One of Israel, your Saviour." Isaiah 43: 1-3*

Finally, the much eagerly awaited all clear siren filled the air, much to our relief, to signal the departure of enemy planes. As we came out from our hiding place, unscathed, I truly believed there was someone more powerful than Kuan Yin and He is my God of miracles who had snatched us from the jaws of death.

We were anxious to assess the damages inflicted by the enemy planes on our quarters. To our surprise, in spite of the heavy bombing, there was not the slightest damage to our house. The wall clock, picture frames and glass mirrors were unmoved and there were no visible cracks on the walls either. You can see how solid the police building must have been. Still, we were quite curious to know the condition of the other parts of the building. So we opened our glass windows. To my horror the moment the windows were opened, I saw nothing but palls of thick, black clouds of heavy smoke drifting and billowing towards my face. So dense was the smoke that it completely blanketed the large parade quadrangle in front of us, and the administrative block beyond as well. Thus, we saw nothing but plumes of floating dark smoke with its heavy stifling fumes of burning sulphur, blowing into our houses. So nauseous was the smoke that I almost puked had my cousin not shut the windows quickly.

Just then, my uncle rushed home, panting as he shouted to my aunt, "Pack up all your valuables immediately! Gather up some rice, dried noodles and whatever canned food available and some clothes quickly. We are leaving the house now and the police jeep is coming shortly to pick us up!" Soon the police jeep arrived at our doorstep with a police driver and we scrambled hurriedly into the police vehicle but I had no idea where we were going. I believed only my uncle and aunt had known of this contingency plan.

It was about noon when we sped off from our quarters. As we turned into a stretch of Penang Road, I saw the entire Chowrasta Market and its immediate stretch of shop houses facing the administrative block of the Police Headquarters engulfed in flames. The enemy had rained hundreds of highly inflammable bombs indiscriminately during the air strike. Tongues of leaping orange flames flickered skyward from the burning inferno but they were easily swallowed up by the hungry black smoke hovering above and streaking across the pale skyline of Georgetown. I also witnessed fire fighters frantically engaged to fight the raging inferno around the market. Ambulances with sirens blaring all the way were dashing to the rescue of the many injured and dying. Never had I witnessed such chaos on the streets caused by the ravages of war.

While we were still on the road, another air raid sounded to alert us of approaching enemy planes. We stopped just in front of the Dhoby Ghaut Market, which is near the General Hospital. The driver pulled up immediately and all of us quickly jumped into the 4 to 5 feet deep monsoon drain for cover. As we crouched low and clutching tightly to our precious belongings, we soon heard the monotonous drones of the enemy planes over our heads. I prayed that the enemy would not pick the hospital as their target, for we were just hiding close by, lest stray bombs might fall on us. Soon after, the planes drifted further away without any more strikes. The all clear siren came on, and we hurriedly continued on our journey towards a remote rubber plantation in a rural area, outside Georgetown, and arrived at a small brick house.

I am unable to provide the detail of this location as I do not have the resources to verify this location. This was a small, one-storey brick building, quite way off the main road. Later, I came to understand from conversations among the adults, that this house belonged to a senior expatriate police officer and his family for their safe retreat, in the event of war. There was also a freshly dug air raid shelter in front of the house. It was six feet deep with several small roots of rubber trees left protruding from the sides of the shelter, the earthen floor of which was rough and damp. It still puzzles me as to how my uncle, at most, the chief clerk in the Police Headquarters, or maybe, the private secretary to the Chief Police Officer, could have access to a police jeep and his house for our evacuation.

Nothing untoward occurred on the first day but the second day, in the middle of the night, we were awakened by the blast of the air raid siren. "Wake the children!" shouted my uncle to my aunt, "Don't switch on the lights!" In the quiet of the night, we were rudely awakened and ushered out of the house towards the air raid shelter, with my uncle leading the family with a dimmed torch light. Sam Ku Cheh was holding me by my hand, when suddenly I wanted to take a leak so I asked to be allowed to run to the bathroom. "Leak?" she hissed sarcastically, "Leak your silly head! When I don't wake you up, you don't leak; now when I wake you up, you want to leak!" and with that remark she gave me two sharp slaps on my sleepy head and pulled me into the air raid shelter. I momentarily lost my urge to leak but when it came on again, I had to criss-cross my legs to subdue the urge. This time we did not hear the enemy planes as we crouched inside the air raid shelter. After an hour or so of anxiety in the darkness of the pit, finally, the all clear siren came on much to our relief and we headed for the house.

That was to be my last brush with air raids. After a couple of days in this brick house, the next thing I remembered was that my uncle moved the family to stay in a rented Malay hut in Paya Terubong some distance away from the Air Itam market. It was safe to move out because the Japanese forces had successfully occupied Penang. The people were encouraged to return to their homes and shopkeepers were forced to reopen their shops. This was to be the beginning of a new way of life for the population under Japanese rule for the first time.

# The Malay Hut in the village of Paya Terubong, Air Itam

# Circa Dec 1941 – June 1942

It was to this Malay kampong house in Paya Terubong built on stilts, that my uncle brought his mistress, Luk Ku and her family to live with us, all under one roof. Luk Ku, had by now, bore my uncle a baby daughter and the two families seemed happily reconciled. My uncle, a very loyal British subject, was very anti-Japanese and hated the Japanese for breaking his rice bowl. He was more so, when one evening upon returning home, he narrated to us how he was unceremoniously slapped by a Japanese foot soldier for not bowing properly to him in deference, when he was passing through a barbed road block barricade guarded by him. As my uncle would not work for the Japanese, there was no family income then. So, I believed both my aunty and Luk Ku must have been pawning their jewelleries to feed four adults (including Luk Ku's babysitter) and 6 children.

The hut with two bedrooms and a wall was sparsely furnished. All the six children and the babysitter slept in the hall. Pre-war coal-fired stoves were replaced by make-shift stoves of loose stone slabs and fuelled by dried twigs and leaves instead of charcoal or firewood. The job of collecting the latter fell on my shoulders every day with the occasional help from the babysitter, if circumstances permitted. I would be shirtless as I scoured the neighbouring village with a parang to look out for dried leaves and branches. I would cut the twigs and branches to appropriate lengths and drag these back to our house to be dried for fuel. This was a very trying task for me as I had no previous experience. However, I was fortunate to be spared from helping to dig our well for drinking water and for baths for the adults for there came along a male bachelor friend of my uncle, Tse Liang, who was to help in such menial jobs in exchange for board and lodging.

Tse Liang who was in his thirties was quite a shrewd character. One morning, I was called by Luk Ku to sell fried noodles which my 3rd paternal aunt cooked, in the Air Itam market. This was supposedly to help supplement the family's income and Tse Ling was to accompany as the "manager". So around eight in the morning, we both trudged to the market with the pot of fried noodles and a basket containing the plates and chopsticks. We managed to find a shady spot close to the market to set up our business. We had neither tables nor chairs for customers, but we found a rough slab of stone to sit on, to rest our tired legs. By noon, we only had five customers and the morning shade was slowly losing its desired effect. Tse Liang decided to call it a day and wanted to go home for lunch in spite of the loss but I pleaded with him to stay on a bit longer lest I might be reprimanded by the two women for the poor sales.

Tse Liang reassured me that it was lunch time and people would be eating at home. Besides, the noodles were getting cold. "It would be better to lose money from the start. If we have made a profit, you'll be selling fried noodles every day in the market. I pity you, do you understand?" he reasoned with me. And as I hesitated to ponder over his reasoning, he repeated the word, "every day!" so emphatically. He sounded quite logical and I was taken in by him so we packed up to go home. While on the way, I began to realise that he, too, would be spared, if my aunt and Luk Ku were to really call off the project. "Oh how smart of him," I thought. We eventually explained with sad faces to the women that we just did not have enough customers.

They accepted our pathetic story and decided to abort the noodles project permanently, much to our delight!

Months passed by and without any family income, I believed Sam Ku Cheh must have pawned all her jewellery to buy food. The whole family had to depend on the wealthy Luk Ku to feed us as she possessed more jewellery than my aunt. So she was now the one holding the reins of the family expenses as she doled out the daily housekeeping money to my aunt to do the marketing, giving her instructions about what to buy and cook for the family. Thus, we could see Luk Ku usurping the position of mistress of the house from my aunt, who had become dependent on her. Luk Ku was to become our benefactor and provider while my aunt was reduced to that of a servant, taking orders from her supposedly "younger sister" – a position not only embarrassing but very painful to her as she had lost her pride of place in the house.

Angry with herself, she could not vent her frustrations on my uncle nor her children. So she exploded all her pent up emotions on me, scolding me for no apparent reason or chiding me for my little mistakes. She called me names like "good for nothing, useless bum, a jinx" and so on, a daily occurrence which I had to bear in silence. It was also embarrassing too especially when such verbal abuses were within ear shot of everyone including my cousins and their two small step sisters. Initially, my cousins were apathetic to their mother's tantrums but as those daily verbal abuses protracted from days to weeks, they became sympathetic to me. They soon mustered enough courage to become empathetic brokers between their mother and me. I was really touched by their initiative as they comforted me. As tears began to well up in my eyes, I tried to remain stoic. But when it became unbearable, I had to hide myself behind the well to cry silently. There were times that I had wanted to run away to avoid my aunt's cruel taunts. But at the same time, I knew she was by nature not the aggressive type and acknowledged that she had always been kind and generous towards me in the past. Just blame it on the current circumstances, I comforted myself.

But there came an incident later that was to change my life and to remain in the house was no longer an option. It was wont of me every morning to boil water and fill up the thermos flask. Everyone knew my daily routine. Early that particular morning, while everyone was still sleeping and after I had filled the thermos flask with hot water, I then placed it on the table. Little did I realise that I had put the thermos flask on top of my cousin's spectacles, and broke it. On awakening and discovering his spectacles had been cracked, he shouted at me and scolded me angrily. Luckily for me, both his parents were out but I knew I would be in great trouble when they got home. That incident was the last straw as panic soon gripped me. Knowing my uncle's fiery and quick temper and my aunt's dislike for me, I expected a severe tongue-lashing from them and a possible beating. On the spur of the moment, and on my own volition, I decided to propel myself out of the house as if there was no tomorrow. Where to go then? The only refuge for me was to return to 15 Amoy Lane to be with my Koo Mah and my siblings. I knew the life there would be more difficult and desperate and it would be like jumping out of the frying pan into the fire. Still I hastily grabbed some of my belongings and without a word to anybody, I left knowing fully well that the road ahead would be a rocky one. This was to be the longest journey on foot of my entire life, a 15 mile walk from Paya Terubong to Amoy Lane. Approximately 2 miles down the road, my uncle and aunt caught up with me in their car after honking at me from behind, they did not stop though and drawing up close to me, my aunt just wagged her finer angrily at me as if to warn me to be careful and drove off. Shrugging off my fatigue, I continued my slow walk on the tortuous road, resigned myself to a new life of struggles and hardships as I headed to 15 Amoy Lane.

While on the road, it suddenly dawned on me that the servant also could have removed the thermos flask to prepare milk for the infant early in the morning. She could have placed it on top of the spectacles and thus be the one who broke the spectacles – not me. I could be exonerated and blameless. Oh, forget it, I mused to myself. The waste was already under the bridge.

# 15 Amoy Lane
## Circa: 1942 – 1943

I was already 13 years old when I returned to join Ku Ma and my siblings permanently at the above address, after having stayed with Sam Ku Cheh for five years. As mentioned earlier in my preceding chapters, my relationship with my siblings was already not close. So upon my return, it was initially rather difficult for me to establish good rapport with them.

Let me highlight some very interesting anecdotes of my chronicles during my stay here. First, let me introduce to you what was known as the much dreaded "Sook Ching" (a military exercise practised by the Japanese Imperial Forces to pick out men suspected of being British spies). One morning, Japanese soldiers armed with loud speakers going from street to street, ordered all males, 12 years old and above, to come out of their houses to a designated spot. We were ordered to squat down in four rows outside a row of terrace houses. We had to remain quiet and to look up straight. Two of my good neighbours, Ewe Hock and Jimmy, in their early thirties squatted just behind me.

As I craned my neck to look left and right to see what was going on, I suddenly spotted a man in ski mask slowly walking down the road towards us. Walking right behind this mysterious man, were two or three burly soldiers carrying rifles. Scrutinizing closely at the people squatted and facing him, he suddenly stopped in front of us, panning his eyes from left to right. In dead silence, we all watched with our hearts in our mouths. Slowly, the hooded guy raised his hand and pointed his finger towards my spot! Immediately the three accompanying soldiers waded in past me and grabbed my neighbours, Ewe Hock and Jimmy, much to our astonishment! My neighbours resisted and protested vehemently to no avail, as they were slapped and dragged unceremoniously and driven to the infamous Kempetai (Military Police) HQ. It was unbelievable that my neighbours were accused of being British spies. Had they been mistakenly identified? Was there a grudge between them and this informer, the hooded guy? I had known them for years as ordinary salesmen of clothes and toiletries. Ewe Hock and his wife Pow Chee, had taken me out for picnics with their children in the past. You can well imagine Pow Chee's reaction when she was informed of this arrest. I was told she fainted. The Kempetai were noted for their cruel tortures to extract information from the detainees! Many failed to come out alive from the torture chambers. Pow Chee and her family must have invested a fortune on the many intermediaries to get both of them freed or get a chance to visit them. But, all their attempts were hopelessly in vain.

To cut the story short, Ewe Hock and Jimmy were very lucky to return home safely after months of torture. But they were literally reduced to skin and bones. Grapevine had it that they had been subjected to water treatment almost daily, whereby water would be forced into their mouths through rubber tubes. The soldiers would cruelly stomp their heavy boots on their bloated stomachs to force out the water. Very often, they would be hung upside down in the open sunny yard, to be beaten with heavy poles, until they confessed or fainted, and left dangling under the hot and burning sun. It was a miracle that they survived the torture, and returned safely home to their loved ones.

Now, for the second narrative.

*"Yiu char kueh, yiu char kueh*
*Yiu char kueh, jua-jua*
*Jua-jua, yiu char kueh"*

This is a refrain that I used to chant as I made my debut as a street hawker selling hot yiu char kueh at the age of 4. Yiu char kueh is the Hokkien (Chinese dialect) name of two-piece elongated cake (about 12 inches), made from wheat four. It is deep fried, and lots of people enjoy it with a cup of coffee or eat it with porridge for breakfast. "Jua-jua" is the Hokkien word for "hot". My younger brother, Peng Yew, aged 10, had already been selling it for the past few months, earning about 3 Japanese yen each day, from the sale of 30 pieces of yiu char kueh. I condescended to join my brother on this job to support Ku Ma and my sisters. Peng Yew demonstrated to me the way to shout "Yiu char kueh" the refrain, which I then practiced repeatedly to get used to it. We had to wake up by 5 o'clock at the break of dawn to queue among other street vendors at the yiu char kueh stall. We felt very uncomfortable in the cold, almost shivering, especially if we were at the far end of the long queue, but we would feel warmer as we snaked closer towards the hot, burning stove, where the stall owner was preparing and frying the yiu char kueh. I started with just twenty pairs of the yiu char kueh in my basket, and that would hopefully give me a net profit of 2 Japanese yen. Being not used to hawking on the streets, I felt very bizarre, as I was initially shy to cry out the yiu char kueh refrain on the roads. No pain, no gain, as the adage goes. So, fighting off my shyness, I belted out,

*"Yiu char kueh, yiu char kueh*
*Yiu char kueh, jua-jua*
*Jua-jua, yiu char kueh"*

as I trudged along the empty streets, hoping to wake up some potential customers from their cosy beds. Up and down the quiet streets, I continued to "sing" my chorus, "Yiu char kueh jua-jua. Jua-jua yiu char kueh!" 10 minutes, 15 minutes, 20 minutes ticked by slowly without any reward. Did I hear a voice calling me from behind? I looked around but there was no one in sight. I must have been hopelessly hallucinating for my first customer. Finally, a female voice beckoned me towards her. I saw a figure waving at me, and this was real. It was after some thirty minutes that I got my first sale of two pairs of the hot, crispy yiu char kueh. But sales were rather slow in coming. My throat was getting hoarse after repeated calls of my refrain. My legs were beginning to feel tired as I covered additional streets and the morning sun was making me feel hot and bothered. I knew I must finish selling all my wares, and not let Ku Ma down even how tired I might be. It was indeed a hard life, just to earn a meagre sum to eke out a hand-to-mouth living. As days passed by and as I was slowly getting used to it, I gradually increased my quota to 30 pairs of yiu char kueh, even though it would mean longer hours toiling on the streets, but I would be getting an extra Japanese yen for my hard work.

Now, for my third anecdote. While my brother and I were hawking yiu char kueh, a nonya widow, living just a couple of doors from our house, enquired whether we would be interested to hawk her nonya kueh in the afternoons for a commission. She had already commissioned two Indian vendors to sell her kueh. These vendors would balance on their heads, a large round wooden tray, filled with a variety of kueh, as they hawk along the streets. Ku Ma encouraged us to give it a try, as we were quite free in the afternoons. We told the widow that we did not have the skill to balance the heavy round tray on our heads. "Don't worry," replied the widow. "I'll provide you with a 3-tier rattan basket with about 40 to 50 pieces of kueh, on consignment. I'll pay you a commission on the sale and you return me all unsold kueh." It was quite a reasonable proposal and did not involve any capital on our part, just our labour.

So, off to the streets, once again I roamed, carrying the 3-tier basket in the crook of my arm. The new refrain this time was;

> *"Kueh Ko Sui, Kueh Ko Chi,*
> *Kueh Beng Ka, Pulut Tai Tai,*
> *Pulut Inti, Rempah Udang"*

These are cakes all made from glutinous rice in a variety of ways, and with colourings of different shades and fillings; e.g. Rempah Udang wrapped with banana leaves, is filled with some spicy shrimps. But unwittingly, I changed it to sound "Lampah udang," (meaning "shrimps' testicles" in Hokkien) in chanting my refrains! Being Cantonese I did not realize my misnomer.

Sale of these nonya kueh was quite a breeze, but still I sweated in the hot afternoons. I would usually bring home about 3 Japanese yen each day. But, there was one unforgettable incident that I want to share with you. There was this Chinese lady who bought six to eight pieces of kueh. Unwrapping the banana leaf wrappers, she would gobble them up so quickly that I had to make an equally quick count mentally of the discarded wrappers, to determine the number of kueh she had actually consumed. "How much?" she asked, as she wiped her oily lips with the back of her hand. "4 yen," I replied confidently. "Did I eat that much?" she growled, as if in disbelief. "Sure," I countered, and counted for her the wrappers, one by one, as evidence. The skinny woman grudgingly paid me 3 yen. "I owe you 1 yen. Tomorrow you come, I'll pay you. OK?" Reluctantly, I had to accept the 3 yen. So, when I handed over the day's takings to the nonya widow, I had to top it up with 1 yen of my own. Then, on the following day, I called on the skinny woman, who was in fact a prostitute, and asked for the 1 yen she owed me. As usual, she picked several pieces of kueh, as if she had skipped lunch. I was quite happy for this brisk sale. But to my dismay, the wretch again paid me all but 1 yen, and said she would pay me the 1 yen the next day. "Don't be afraid. I cannot run away," she said cheekily. I was very angry with her. I had in mind to tell her to put back all the kueh she had taken, but I also rarely got any customer to buy that many pieces of kueh at any one time. I decided to trust her and once again, I had to make good the shortfall to the nonya widow. Ku Ma suggested that I did not fall for her trickery again and just get back the 1 yen. To my surprise, when I made my call to the brothel the following day, I was told she had moved house! I just shook my head in silent dismay, and vowed to sell my kueh on a cash-on-delivery basis in future.

Next came another change of occupation.

Around this time, I came across a Chinese housewife, who was among one of my regular nonya kueh customers. One day while buying kueh from me, she said, "I observe you have good manners. I think hawking kueh will not bring you much income, even in the future. Why don't you try to learn a skill, like repairing refrigerators? My husband can teach you, if you are interested. I can pay you a monthly allowance of 60 yen with food and accommodation. Would you consider it?" Ku Ma thought it was a good idea to learn a skill for my future. So, I gave up both my street hawker's jobs to become an apprentice-mechanic in refrigerator repairs. Little did I realise that as an apprentice I had also to sweep the home and other parts of the house. For months, I learned very little from my boss, except to wash the bolts and nuts, learn to tighten and loosen screws, and so on. Also I did not like the smell of the ammonia gas used in the refrigerators. As I discovered I had very little interest in this training after all, I then terminated my apprenticeship just after six months on this job.

A chance of going back to school came along. Schools had already been re-opened and children were beginning to study Nihon-go, the Japanese language. I was keen to learn this foreign language which might become useful to me in future if the Japanese were to occupy Malaya permanently. So, with Ku Ma's consent, off to school, I went. I started at the elementary level. I picked up the language very fast, and in the span of six months, I was promoted to the intermediary and later the advanced level, with praises from the Japanese school principal.

While I was at school in the morning, I had lots of free time in the afternoon. One day, it was by chance that I bumped into an ex-Penang Free School classmate, who worked as a newspaper vendor in the afternoon. He had been selling newspapers for the past eight months already and could get a profit of 8 Japanese Yen for every 10 copies sold. After getting Ku Ma's approval, I became a newspaper vendor after school. Initially, I started selling 30 copies of the local newspaper, "Pei Nam Yat Po" (Penang Daily), and after a week later, I took 40 copies from the printing press. Many vendors would cycle off very quickly to sell their stuff, while others, like me, would run as fast as we could to hit the road, carrying our loads under our arms, shouting "Pei Nam Yat Po! Pei Nam Po!" from street to street to attract our customers. It was very tiring, carrying a heavy load of newspapers under my arms, but it was worth the discomfort, knowing the pain would bring me some gain of about 25 Japanese yen each day, for my Ku Ma.

During this time, I had a surprise lady visitor from Seremban, the capital of the state of Negeri Sembilan. She was none other than Ku Ma's foster daughter, Madam Lee Swee Pin. She and her husband were the couple who had vacated their front room at 35 Ariffin Road, for Luk Ku to move in. She had since been divorced and had been supporting herself as a dance hostess in Kuala Lumpur ever since. Later, when Japan occupied Malaya, she became a kept mistress of a high ranking Japanese army officer, Colonel Doshi, the garrison commander based in Seremban. When she came to know of my proficiency in the Japanese language, she suggested that the Japanese commander might be able to use his influence to get me a decent job, if I were ready to go to Seremban. Ku Ma had no objection to the said proposal and off I proceeded to Seremban with my cousin, Madam Lee, quite apprehensively unaware of what my future would be. But, God had assured me not to worry. We learn from the Bible that even the birds, who do not sow or reap, are being fed by God. So, are we not of more value than the birds? (Luke 12: 22-24) So, why am I apprehensive? I have the Lord Jesus Christ as my shepherd, who gives his life for his sheep, even for those who are outside his fold. (John 10: 11; 16) Assured by God's word, I proceeded to continue my cruise of faith to the unknown, Seremban!

# Dan Ji Shi Han Gakko Seremban (Men's' Teacher Training College Circa 1943 – 1945)

"You will be known as Lee Low," Madam Lee said to me. "I'll introduce you to the garrison commander as my younger brother to avoid unnecessary explanations. So you take after my surname, understand?" Thus I became known as 'Lee Low', even without a deed poll! Lt. Col. Do Shi was in his 50s and did not have the appearance of an aggressive officer. Neither was he aloof and was easily approachable. He occupied a large mansion, the legacy of a high ranking colonial official. I was provided a room downstairs next to his valet soldier who was quite friendly to me. It was rather difficult initially to understand him, for spoken Japanese is quite different from the formal grammar of written Japanese that I learned in school. While staying here, I had my first taste of Japanese food, including eating raw fish – sashimi. I failed to get work because of my tender age of 14. However, I was assured by the commander that in a month or two, there would be a new Teacher Training College in Seremban, and he could get me enrolled, if I was interested to become a teacher. On successful completion of the one year intensive course, I would be teaching Nihon-go.

When the College was finally ready to take in the first batch of trainers, I was driven there in the commander's car. After making some enquiries, the driver escorted me to see the principal who must have been expecting me judging by their conversation. I went through the interview with the principal and had my proficiency in Nihon-go assessed. I passed the test and was accepted as a trainee. To my surprise, I seemed to be the youngest among the forty recruits whose average age was twenty. There were only 3 Chinese, 3 Indians and the rest were Malays. The training was very tough physically. We had to get up at about 5.30 am to begin the day with light callisthenics, followed by long jogs along the streets. I was surprised that I could cope with this morning drill although I was aching all over initially. We had three square meals each day with fruits and desserts too.

Courses of study included Nihon-go, Mathematic, Japanese culture, History and Music in the mornings and in the afternoons we had to do gardening from 4.00 – 6.00 pm. Twice a week, we were given training in gymnastics which I was completely hopeless at. I dreaded gymnastics as I simply could not master even the basic movements like 'chin-up' on the horizontal bar and leap frogging over the padded horse when every one could do it so effortlessly. That often made me the butt of their endless practical jokes. Of the various gymnastic equipment, I hate the padded or vaulting horse the most, where the participant had to leap frog over it with both legs spread wide open. I could never successfully jump over it to land with both my feet firmly on the ground when everyone could. Some could even do a somersault over the horse so gracefully but I would with legs wide open, land sitting on top of it and painfully bruising my groin every time I brushed against the rough edges of the horse. My silly stance on top of the horse would bring laughter and jeers from the boys, much to my embarrassment. Shaking his head as he observed my frustrations, the gym instructor finally excused me and spared me the misery. I continued to do the callisthenics though, as it did not pose any problems to me.

Do you know how the Japanese extort confessions from the criminals? In my college it was a 'slug fest' involving all forty trainees. The kitchen staff reported that there had been a spate of banana thefts from the locked kitchen store room and the lecturers had concluded that the trainees were the culprits. So one afternoon, a special roll call was summoned and we assembled in front of Mr Kato, the principal. We were surprised to see him carrying his Samurai sword. As we were wondering why this extraordinary roll call, an angry Kato Sensei announced, "Someone has been stealing bananas from the kitchen. Now will the thief or thieves step forward?" We were stunned. No wonder he was carrying his sword for the first time. I thought it was to cut off the hands of the thief!

There was dead silence in the hall as we looked at each other, standing in columns of four by ten. When none came forward, he bellowed angrily, "Now for the last time, come out!" While the innocent ones looked around for signs of any movement, I believed the guilty ones must be scared stiff and shivering at the sight of Kato Sensei's sword. No one showed the slightest movement.

"All right then, listen to me," ordered Kato Sensei. As we were standing in four rows of ten in each row, he instructed that we turn to face each other. At his command of "Strike 1", boys in rows 1 and 3 were to punch those in rows 2 and 4 on the cheek respectively, and "Strike 2" would signal rows 2 and 4 to do likewise to those in rows 1 and 3.

What a shock to us! Many of us were going to be hit and punished in spite of our innocence. "Strike 1" came and I got one hard blow on my cheek from my partner. It was quite painful. Then came "Strike 2" and I gave one back to my partner with great relish. No sign of the culprit or culprits appearing. So "Strike 1" came loud and clear and I got another one punch from my partner but I was smart to turn up my face slightly away from the blow to reduce the impact as it was about to land on my cheek, but still my cheek smarted from the impact. When "Strike 2" was called, I hit him just as hard as he had struck me. I saw his cheek and ear flushing red and I believed mine were just as bad. The third round would be disastrous, I thought. When will this slug fest stop? I wondered. Suddenly, a voice in Malay rang out. The Head Boy pleaded with those responsible for the thefts to surrender. Sure enough, immediately, two Malay boys stepped out to confess their crimes and the slug fest ended abruptly. Fuming with rage, Kato Sensei punched and slapped them repeatedly when they stepped on the platform where he had been waiting so impatiently. With the sword still inside its scabbard, he used it to rain heavy blows on their bare backs. How they sobbed and screamed in pain. I was really scared that he might cut off their fingers too knowing his violent temper. After a stern warning, he eventually dismissed us, leaving us smarting from the unforgettable ordeal.

On one occasion, I too had a very narrow escape from corporal punishment by Kato Sensei. Our College would occasionally practise fire drills in the middle of the night, following which, all trainees would be led to march and jog along the streets, as a show of our discipline and intensive training. We also noted in the course of our training, that such stunts would sometimes occur especially when Mr Kato had returned to the College, from his visits to the Bangsawan opera in the amusement park. So there was this night while I was deep in sleep, I dreamed that I heard many voices calling out numbers simultaneously, 'ichi, ni, san, shi, go (one, two three, four, five) and so on. Then I heard, "Mo ikkai!" (one more time) from another sharp voice of authority. So as the calling of numbers was being repeated, it seemed to me that the cacophonies of voices were getting louder and clearer. I slowly opened my eyes as I was by now awakened. To my horror, these voices echoing from the field below my dormitory were real and I knew at once that it was no dream after all.

The lights in my dorm were on and the beds all around me were empty. Then, I heard a prefect reporting "Hitori inai" (one absent). "Dare Da?" barked Mr Kato angrily. "Lee Low desu" (It's Lee Low) came the quick reply. Oh my goodness! I realised that the fire drill exercise was in progress and I was the only one who had not responded to the drill. What should I do? In despair, I tried to think of a reasonable excuse but before I decided on one, suddenly, I saw Yusof sensei, a lecturer step into my dorm quietly. "Nan da Lee Low?" (What is the matter, Lee Low?) he asked. "Byoki desu!" (I'm sick), I uttered spontaneously without hesitation. Mr. Yusof gestured to me to join the assembly immediately. Now that I had given this excuse, I knew that I had to stick to it. I quickly put on my uniform and shoes and rushed to the field to face Mr Kato's wrath. "Taiken shitsurei shmashita, Kato Sensei." (I'm very sorry Mr Kato) I began but he cut me short. "Nan da?" (Why?) he shouted angrily at me. "Byoki desu," (I am sick) I said sheepishly. Will my bluff work? It must work or else he would scare the daylights out of me. Then Mr Kato surprisingly gestured to Mr Yusof although there were other lecturers close by to check if I really had fever. My fate was now in the hands of this local teacher. I was beginning to have cold sweat as Mr Yusof slowly approached me nonchalantly. He placed his hand on my cold and perspiring forehead. I was on tenterhooks when Mr Yusof approached Mr Kato to report, saying, "Lee Low wa honto byoki desu. (Lee Low indeed is sick) Atama ga atsui desu." (His head is warm). I could hardly believe my ears. It was so nice of Mr Yusof to collude with me. I could not thank him enough for sticking to me through thick and thin. "Whether you're sick or not, you must fall in to be counted in case of a fire, you will be roasted," roared Mr Kato. "Hai Kashikomari mashita," (yes, I understand respectfully) I said and bowed to him reverently. While I returned to my dormitory with much relief to relax and ponder over my ordeal, I noticed Mr Kato leading the staff and my poor colleagues on their usual jogging routine down the streets to the chorus of "ichi, ni, ichi ni." (one, two, one, and two….). Eventually the voices faded so gently and I could return to my slumber.

Here is another interesting anecdote of my training. One day Mr Kato announced to us that the State Information Department was organising an elocution contest open to all students in institutions of higher learning and urged us to participate. In the process, our

College submitted four entries, Zakaria, Arshad, Annamalai and me. We prepared our speeches. The title of my speech was "Nihon No Arawashi." (The Japanese Eagles). I was not referring to the birds of prey but the formidable Japanese Air Force. In my speech, I highlighted the prowess of the Japanese pilots for their sinking of the two powerful British warships, The Prince of Wales and Repulse off the coast of Malaya at the start of the war. These battleships were the pride of the British Navy sent to fortify Malaya. Kato Sensei put his heart and soul to drill us and gave us lots of practices as he rehearsed with us almost every alternate day. On the eve of the competition, he tried to allay our stage fright. To remain calm, he suggested that we write the character 'hito' (people) on our palm with our finger and then 'swallow' it. By doing so we would have 'swallowed up the audiences' and would be speaking to an empty wall.

"Kui ban me! Ni hon no arawasi" announced the Master of Ceremony. (Contestant number 9 – The Japanese Eagles). Yes, it was my turn to speak. Quickly, I pressed my palm with the imaginary word 'people' on it to my mouth and 'swallowed' up all the audiences to contain my stage fright. Up on the stage I went, bowed stiffly to the huge Hino Maru flag serving as the backdrop, as did all the other contestants before me, then another deep bow facing the audience. Adjusting the microphone, I began, "Mina san, watashi no hanashi wa, Ni Hon No Arawasi to imas" (Ladies and gentlemen, the title of my speech is "The Japanese Eagles") I was calm indeed and spoke with confidence after so much coaching and rehearsing by Kato Sensei. No stuttering, whatsoever. I neither missed any word nor was I forced to look at my script. I was very satisfied with my performance and I believed I received the loudest applause. Zakaria, my closest rival, who proceeded before me was unfortunate, in that he faltered at one stage and was forced to read his script. That unfortunately ruined his chances, otherwise, he would be in the running for a prize. After all the 25 contestants had delivered their speeches, it was time for the announcement of the results for which we were eagerly waiting. There were five awards to be given.

After the fifth, fourth, third, and runner up had received their prizes, the rest of us were waiting with great anticipation, wondering who would emerge as the champion. The MC continued, "and the champion is…" he slowly announced to keep us in suspense, "Kiu ban me, Ni Hon no Arawasi – Lee Low!" (Number 9 – The Japanese Eagles – Lee Low). I jumped in jubilation at the announcement, as my fellow contestants congratulated me sportingly. Soon many of my course mates seated just behind me surged round me, patting me on my shoulders as they shared my joy. I was indeed on cloud nine. By becoming the inaugural state elocution champion, I did both Mr Kato and the College proud. For my effort, I received a silver trophy cup and 50 Japanese yen from the Head of the Education Department.

I eventually graduated from the Dan Ji Shi Han Gakko after a year's intensive training. Zakaria was the top student, I came out second in the overall ranking and together with Shaari, who was third, and we both were appointed lecturers to serve in our alma mater. Our College was later renamed Rensei Dojo, a residential college specially tasked with the retraining of current school teachers. Therefore, most of the 'students' were much older than me; some were even old enough to be my father! Fortunately, because of the strict discipline enforced by Kato Sensei these teachers gave me a certain degree of respect and showed admiration for my Japanese proficiency.

Here is another interesting chapter of my past as a qualified teacher during this time residing in the College. I was coming to 16, and apart from teaching the language, I also had to carry out the duties of a warden in rotation with other staff. One night, I daringly deserted my post and sneaked out of the College to watch a boxing match in the park. It was the championship fight between two great boxers touted as the Fight of the Year. Tiger Aman, a Malay pugilist described as very fast with both fists and credited with 14 knock-outs was to fight Slogger Ang, a Chinese renowned for his deadly left upper-cuts having floored just as many opponents. I had watched these two great boxers on previous occasions. But of all nights, this championship match was to take place on the same night that I was on warden duty. What a shame! I was determined not to miss this interesting match which I had been anxiously waiting. I asked a colleague, Shaari to swap duties with me but he would not. He advised me to forget about the boxing match lest the Principal discovered that I had sneaked out.

Throwing caution to the wind, I ventured to the park alone hoping to return to my post at the end undetected. The preliminary supporting bouts had already just ended when I arrived at the arena. Next on the card was the championship bout. I waited patiently for the boxers to climb on to the stage. I promised myself that I would cycle back to the College as soon as the fight was over. Suddenly, I saw a group of spectators standing up to cheer Tiger Aman as he was climbing on to the stage and a few moments later another group was clapping very loudly for Slogger Ang as he made his way into the ring. No sooner had the excitement subsided when I felt a soft tap on my shoulder from behind. Turning around, I saw Shaari and I was glad that he had finally changed his mind.

"Hey, Lee Low, you are in deep trouble! Okazaki Sensei, the gym instructor just called me to ask for you. He was wondering why you were not manning the post. I tried to be evasive and gave him some silly excuses but he wanted to know what happened to you. He seemed very angry and wanted you to call him." I could not help but exclaim, "Oh no! I am going to die this time" Shaari urged me to hurry back as quickly as possible lest Mr Okazaki was waiting for me at the post. Mr Okazaki was noted for his quick temper. He had in fact, assaulted Shaari previously in the presence of the trainees for a minor mistake. So we scurried as fast as we could on our bicycles. Shaari being older to me, advised me to return Okazaki's call and apologise to him hoping that he would be appeased. We parted company at the college gate. With my heart in my mouth, I approached my duty room. Noticing that the light was not switched on, I was indeed relieved that Okazaki Sensei had not come to ambush me, after all. Now the big question was whether I should give him a call. I was at sixes and sevens as I sat before the telephone. Finally, I mustered enough courage to face the music, I dialled Okazaki Sensei. "Okazaki Sensei, domo shitsurei aeshita!" (Mr Okazaki, I am very sorry) I began to explain apologetically my folly to watch the boxing contest and immediately, he shouted over the phone, "Bagaro" (You fool). After giving me quite an earful, he warned me not to repeat this folly and simmered down. Sensing that he had softened his stance, I was emboldened to ask him why he had called me earlier. He had always been quite nice to me and said that he wanted me to take over his mathematics class the following day to which I obliged unhesitatingly much to his delight.

Now for another daring episode of my chronicles which exposed another of my imperfections. One morning, I had a surprise visit from my cousin, Chan (son of my second paternal aunt) accompanied by two of his friends. They had sought me for assistance to help them leave Seremban for they were deserters from their para-military camp and they could not cope with the strenuous and rigorous training. They needed temporary shelter and a travel permit to return to Penang quickly, in case they were stopped by Japanese solders at exit points. I agreed to help them and gave them my room which I moved out to sleep with my colleague.

My cousin asked me if I could forge a travel permit for them for he had previously known of my language proficiency. Due to our kinship and after much persuasion, I finally agreed. I was very naïve then, not realising at that time, the danger I was courting. There had to be the official rubber stamp of their camp in order to complete the forged travel permits. I even volunteered to get the stamp for them. I had a crew cut hair style at that time and putting on a white shirt with another khaki one over it and a pair of khaki shorts; I looked very much like a Japanese official. The same day, I approached a rubber stamp engraver and gave him instructions in Japanese laced with faltering disguised Mandarin to carve out the name of the camp. He was so convinced by my ruse that he hastened to do so without any questions. So bringing home the rubber stamp, I wrote for their travel permits, stamped the fake permits and finally attested a fake signature of their camp commander to complete the whole process. What an audacity!

At the young age of under 16 years, I had already committed a crime of forgery risking my neck for my cousin and his friends. I could hardly sleep that night as I began to realise the seriousness of my crime. I even dreamt that I was dragged from my bed by a group of Kempeitai (Military Police) who tortured me and the three AWOLS. Down came the samurai sword on my neck!!! I woke up abruptly with the sun shining into my room. What a nightmare! I wanted to persuade my cousin to abort their plan which would surely incriminate me if any one of them was caught. I discovered they had already left my room. I quickly opened my wardrobe for a quick change of clothes but to my bitter dismay, I found that they had stolen three pairs of my trousers leaving their dirty ones inside. What rascals these deserters turned out to be. This proved that the adage, "A good turn deserves another," is not necessarily true. With arms akimbo, I wondered aloud, "How could these scoundrels do such a thing to me? Risking my neck for them and yet they had the gall to steal from me. Wait till I catch up with them."

On hindsight, now that they had changed into civilian clothes, the trio should have aborted using the forged document and besides, travelling as civilians, they did not need to have travel permits.

Furthermore, it would not be wise for them to produce permits with their names written on them for their commander would have reported their desertion to the appropriate authorities to look out for them. For the next few days, I was certainly worried to death hoping and praying for their safety lest I be incriminated, if they were apprehended. I really thanked God for His compassion to protect me in spite of my transgression.

As the war raged on, Allied Forces were slowly defeating the Japanese in many battle fronts and regaining many of their lost territories. Now Tokyo was within easy reach of American B-29 bombers as America had occupied some neighbouring islands belonging to Japan. In early August, 1945, America dropped its first atomic bomb on Hiroshima and three days later, followed by another bomb on Nagasaki killing hundreds of thousands of innocent Japanese civilians. On 15 August, Japan finally surrendered to the Allied armed forces. (Agreement formally signed on 2 September 1945)

Meanwhile, British planes began to drop pamphlets all over Malaya heralding the impending return of the British Armed Forces with occasional bombing of Japanese strategic installations. There was no denying that the Japanese would be leaving soon. One morning, Kato Sensei assembled us just outside his office and we wondered why he approached us in full uniform with his samurai sword hanging loosely by his side. He appeared pale and solemn. We bowed to him when one of our staff members gave the command and clicking his heels together Kato Sensei saluted us in return. He began to address us slowly and stoically, "You must have known by now that Japan has lost the war and has surrendered," his voice choking with emotion. He struggled on as he looked straight into our eyes. "I'm very sorry to have brought so much hardship to all of you all these years. I ask for your forgiveness" then he bowed to each of us one at a time slowly as he shook our hands. We were more than surprised at his humble gesture. He had been a good principal, fair in his judgements, after all. Some of my seniors were already teary-eyed and I could not hold back my tears either. As he stood before me, he held my shoulders, embraced me and nodded his head a couple of times. "Study hard," he whispered. "Yes sir, I will," I answered. "I hope you will return safely to your family", I added. Many years after the war, I came to know that he and Okasaki never made it home for their boat was unfortunately sunk after hitting a sea mine.

When the people came to know that the Japanese troops were leaving, they quickly exchanged their Japanese "Banana currency" for Malayan dollars on the black market. I managed to get some Malayan currency notes in exchange for the few Japanese yen to tide me over temporarily.

Let me go back a little before Mr Kato's sad departure. During the few months just before Japan's surrender, I was allotted living quarters at Lemon Street by the Education Department. But it was still being 'illegally' occupied by a Madam Siow, a widow and her family. Her husband was working for the Japanese but had already died and I was told I could evict the family. There were three bedrooms and as I needed only one, I could not simply ask the Siows to leave. Furthermore, Madam Siow was a widow with a teenaged daughter and two sons. I could not be a dog in the manger. I still remembered my widowed mother's hardships. The Bible tells us to be good to widows, "Learn to do good, seek justice, reprove the oppressor, defend the fatherless, plead for the widow" – Isaiah 1:17. So I allowed them to continue their stay rent free. The Siows were devout Catholics and through them, I was encouraged to attend Mass quite regularly. I even attended weekly Catechism classes and thus once again I came close to knowing Jesus Christ.

Now that the Japanese Imperial Forces had finally been defeated, the country came under the administration of the British Military Administration initially. At the same time, emerging from the

Malayan jungles for the first time was the MPAJA forces (Malayan Anti-Japanese Army), the so-called anti-Japanese guerrillas who had been supporting the British as spying partners and thus sabotaging the enemy. I saw them in action for the first time in their green uniform on the streets of Seremban – in fact, just two doors away from where I was staying. One of their immediate tasks was to ferret out the people who spied for the Japanese and other betrayers too. One afternoon my attention was drawn to the sudden appearance of two military trucks parked at the centre of the road outside my house. Several armed MPAJA soldiers then jumped out and rushed towards a house, two doors away. They ran up the stairs located outside the house in hot pursuit of the fugitive. A large group of curious spectators had gathered to watch the drama. I climbed a low wall to get a closer look. Suddenly soldiers were bringing down the captive from the upper storey of the house. The onlookers gasped in surprise, "The Taiwanese!" they whispered. The fugitive wore a sleeveless singlet and a pair of shorts and his hands were securely bound from behind with ropes, criss-crossed from the front of his chest to his back. He was pale and frightened as if in shock. His pursuers pushed him through the anxious crowds and bundled him into the waiting truck. They then drove off, leaving us wondering what they would do to him.

With the return of the British Military Administration, schools were reopened. After joining Madam Siow's son to study at the St Paul's Institution for a couple of weeks, I began to miss my old school friends in Penang and most importantly my family. Also I could not depend on Madam Siow as she had her own family to support. I had a burning desire to get back to Penang Free School to continue my education. So we parted on a happy note. I took the long train ride to Penang to be reunited with my family at 15, Amoy Lane,

# 15 Amoy Lane
## Circa: Sep 1945 – Dec 1945

Have you ever slept in the kitchen with rodents and cockroaches crawling all over your body? Well, that was precisely where I slept when I returned home from Seremban, after the war had ended. "You're going to sleep in the kitchen," Ku Ma said to me matter-of-factly. "There is no more vacant space in the house for your bed. I'll give you a gunny-sack camp-bed to sleep on." Ku Ma was the chief tenant of this rented house. She was an illiterate spinster. So, how did she manage to find the means to feed my siblings? As chief tenant, she rented out all the bedrooms upstairs, and also leased out a bed-space for an old lady in the second hall downstairs just below the stair case. Whatever available space left, was taken up by my two sisters who had their wooden beds lined up against the wall of the second hall. Ku Ma and my brother had their beds lined up in the main hall against the wall, and on the opposite side of the hall were two mahjong tables and chairs. The mahjong sessions, stretching from morning to late nights, (occasionally right up to the next morning, if all the four players agreed), also provided a second source of income for Ku Ma, through a mahjong "tax" which the players voluntarily agreed to subscribe for the use of the mahjong sets. So cramped was the hall, that one had to walk carefully through the narrow space between the beds and the players, in order not to kick the players'chairs as that would bring bad luck according to the belief of these superstitious players. How could anyone study or sleep in the hall with the cacophony of noises from the shuffling of the plastic mahjong tiles and the raised voices of the losers blaming one another for their losses!

It was unavoidable that I had to sleep in the kitchen. The condition here was not conducive for sleeping and private study. The kitchen light was purposely dimmed, to cut down on the electricity bill. Two chipped wooden dinning tables and stools and three wooden food cabinets occupied much of the space on one side, opposite the stone-stoves. The one and only bathroom for all the 20 householders was located there, and you can say, my sleeping accommodation came with an attached bathroom as compensation for my discomfort.

Do you remember my cousin who approached me in Seremban for help to return to Penang, and together with his friends stole my trousers? Well, one day, I was able to confront him in the house and give him a piece of my mind in the presence of his mother. She was indeed surprised to learn of my sacrifice for him and joined me to castigate him for being so mean and ungrateful. She sympathized with me for her son's ingratitude and willingly sewed a pair of new trousers for me which I gratefully accepted.

On my return to Penang, I lost no time to register for a place in my former school, Penang Free School. I was not too late in my enrolment as schools had just been reopened. I continued to enjoy my fee waiver, which meant very much to me. By the end of the year 1945, all pupils had to sit for the English and Mathematics tests for proper streaming and I was fortunate to be placed in Standard 8A, the following year, 1946.

My school was about seven miles from my house and Ku Ma scrimped to get me a second-hand bicycle for which I was very grateful. I was embarrassed to ask for pocket money, firstly because she was already eking a hand-to-mouth living, and secondly, I was by now 18 years old. As I had to pay my other miscellaneous fees like library and laboratory fees, I gave private tuition to my neighbour's children and those of our close friends living nearby. The money earned was barely enough for my needs.

My living conditions at Amoy Lane were not conducive for my private studies, as I had to suffer the disturbing noises from the mahjong sessions and had to strain my eyes to study because of the dim light in the kitchen. I could only do my homework and private studies when all the householders had finished their dinner and cleared the tables. Even as I sat on the stool to study, I would be distracted by roaches crawling on the table for food and some even crawling up my legs. This situation was so different from the comforts that I fortunately enjoyed while staying with Sam Ku Cheh in the police barracks, only to be interrupted by the war in late 1941.

The only solution to my predicament was to go back to stay with Sam Ku Cheh, for my uncle had been realloted the same living quarters which we had occupied previously. But the big question was how to approach Sam Ku Cheh and my uncle to broach the subject of allowing me to stay with them, knowing too well the previous unpleasant incident of breaking my cousin's spectacles that prompted me to abscond from their house in Paya Terubong. And, besides, I had to contend with my uncle's fiery temper. I had been churning my thoughts over and over again as to how best to approach Sam Ku Cheh on the matter of lodging. After much deliberation, I eventually swallowed my pride and mustered enough courage to broach the subject, which I had been quietly rehearsing by myself, to my aunt. Sheepishly, I pleaded with her, "Ku Cheh, I know I've accidently broken cousin Ming's spectacles. Please forgive me. I find it very difficult to concentrate on my studies in Amoy Lane, as you know. Could you please allow me to come back to stay?" Ku Cheh hesitated for a while as I waited anxiously for her response. She finally gave her approval, very much to my relief. "I can provide you food but no pocket money though," she said. My cousin too was gracious to forgive me and was magnanimous to share his room with me. We were pals again attending the same school and he was one year senior in class to me.

# Police HQ
# Circa: Jan – Dec 1946

There was some improvement in my lifestyle as I returned to stay with Sam Ku Cheh's family, at the beginning of the second term in 1946. God was so gracious to bless me with a forgiving aunt who provided me with a comfortable and conducive home to study. Cousin Ming was very supportive of me too and gave me much help with some of the difficult mathematics questions. He voluntarily lent me his watch for the whole of the duration of the Cambridge Leaving School Certificate Exam, to help me keep time with my papers.

If it had not been for the school free milk scheme, I am sure my studies would have suffered, for there were many occasions when I was penniless. My paltry income derived from giving private tuition was insufficient for my pocket money which was also spent on my other essentials. Very often, I would queue with the junior boys at the canteen for a glass or two of milk to satisfy my hunger pangs, while my friends enjoyed their meals. I did not have the heart to pester Ku Ma for my pocket money as she was already struggling to make ends meet, and the free milk scheme was indeed a blessing. Surely, God is always in control of all things.

My most frustrating episode of my last school days in Penang Free School, was that my classmate, Lee Kum Fatt, received the Additional Mathematics prize, although we both scored 99 marks for that paper in the school examination. I thought we would each be awarded the book prize, but to my bitter disappointment, the prize was to be awarded to my classmate who was just one position above me in the overall marks (according to the school rules). However, I found consolation when I obtained a Grade One Certificate in the

Cambridge School Leaving Certificate Examination at the end of the year, and I received a meritorious cash reward from the school.

Let me describe to you my thrills and excitement in getting my Cambridge results. Our school was the only one privileged to get the results of the Cambridge Certificate Examination one day earlier than the other schools, simply because one of my classmate's father was none other than the managing director of the one and only English newspaper in Penang – "The Straits Echo" which had disclosed that the Education Department would be announcing the results to all schools the following day. So, Khong Guan, my classmate's father surprisingly allowed us to see for ourselves at his office the overall results (the first grades) first hand, sent by the Education Department before sending them for printing. I was among my many friends who trooped to the Straits Echo building that afternoon for the results. There was already a long queue of familiar faces at the information counter, waiting anxiously for their turn. Many went home smiling, as they left the queue and I was among them, when I found "Grade One" printed next to my name.

I was very satisfied with my achievement. Encouraged by my teacher, I applied for admission to study Medicine at the King Edward VII College of Medicine, Singapore and also Arts at the Raffles College, Singapore. Both these tertiary institutions approved my applications, although I was offered dentistry instead of medicine. As I could not afford to further my studies, I happily looked forward for a scholarship to take up one of these two offers. I was very upset and frustrated when I failed in my attempts, and Ku Ma was happy that I could then start to look for work to support the family, instead of waiting for me to complete my tertiary education.

I knew very little about government administration and we did not have career guidance in school. The only occupation I was familiar with was teaching, although my results also qualified me for other occupations like Labour Officer, Immigration Officer and the Settlement Civil Service – all with lucrative start up pay. None of the relatives gave me any advice on these jobs. The only job that I applied successfully was teacher-training, with a monthly allowance of $100. This was a three year teacher-training course during which students attended Saturday morning lectures at the Normal Class, while being attached to a qualified teacher for practical training during weekdays.

# 122-B Hutton Lane

After successfully completing my secondary education, I had the misfortune to move out form the Police Barracks. My uncle had retired by then. Sam Ku Cheh and my cousins stayed in a rented room while my uncle shunted between his wife and mistress daily. Fortunately for me, I was offered food and accommodation by a kind and generous mother of one of my private students living at 122-B Hutton Lane. While staying here, I was already employed as a teacher trainee by the Education Department. While I attended Normal Class every Saturday, I taught at the Westland Primary School during weekdays under the supervision of a qualified teacher. The duration of the training was three years. I failed in my first year most miserably simply because I carelessly answered all four questions when the paper required me to answer two questions only. I was only given marks for the first 2 questions. I passed the theory paper in my following repeat year but I failed the practical teaching this time, despite the help my mentors extended to me in my preparation. My examiner was none other than the Chief Education Officer himself. That ended my teaching career in late November 1951. I had never failed in my tests before so I was very bitter over my failure and cried secretly to myself as my potential rice bowl had just been broken. Many of my teacher associates consoled me, among whom was one by the name of Khoo Soon Teong, a Christian young man married with two little daughters. I was quite attached to this family, often playing chess with him at his home and listening to his music. I also learnt to play tennis from him. He was like a big brother to me, even to this day.

It seemed as if I was not destined to become a teacher and I wondered what other plans God had in store for me. A month later, in December 1951, I chanced upon a government advertisement to recruit social welfare assistants with a starting pay of $75 per month. I noted that my school results matched the required criteria for the post. I submitted my application and was called for an interview in Kuala Lumpur. I prayed to God that would be the "silver lining" to my frustration. While waiting for my turn to be interviewed, Ms Foss, the Training Officer whispered to me that I was over-qualified for the post as the minimum educational qualification was just Standard VIII with credit in English and hinted that I stood a good chance of getting the job. Sure enough, I soon received the official letter of my appointment as a Cadet Social Welfare Assistant and began my career as a social worker from January 1952.

I was initially posted to the Social Welfare office in Penang and was mentored by two senior social welfare assistants. One was a Eurasian and the other a Chinese. I used to ride pillion on their motorcycles during their casework investigations of applicants for public assistance and for admission to aged homes. It was quite an ordeal to be on the Eurasian's motorbike for he was a cigar chain smoker and I had to tolerate the constant flow of the cigar smoke blowing on to my face. After a short spell of understudy, I was relieved to be posted to Kuala Lumpur headquarters for a three month induction course at the conclusion of which I came out top in the examination and was rewarded with an extra salary increment.

After the training, I was then posted to work in the District of Larut and I was based in Taiping, Perak to work under a lady Social Welfare Officer. It was here that I became finally exposed to many forms of social problems including marital problems which I found quite embarrassing as I was still a bachelor and did not even have a girl friend to have experienced any relationship problem. Fortunately,

I could tap on the experiences of a few community leaders, who had volunteered to be arbitrators in the family disputes.

While working in Taiping, I continued to give private tuition to a couple of children for $20 per month in order to supplement my meagre income which amounted to just $160 per month inclusive of living allowance. Still it was a struggle for me to make ends meet as I had to pay $25 per month for my room which was located in the kitchen for economic reasons and I forked out another $70 per month for my lunch and dinner (without breakfast) to the chief tenant. There were times when I had to sacrifice my breakfast or resort to borrowing $10 - $20 from my clerk towards the end of the month. Thus I had very little left to remit to Ku Ma for her maintenance and I really felt pretty bad to appear to be ungrateful to her. I was very hurt by the attitude of the wife of the chief tenant. There was one occasion that I spent about a week's holiday in Penang and brought some money for Ku Ma. I took the opportunity to explain to her my precarious financial situation which she accepted well. When I returned to Taiping, I was surprised when the chief tenant whispered to me that I should get some rebate from his wife for skipping my meals for the past week. I was happy that he was so thoughtful. So one day, he beckoned me to go upstairs. While waiting in the hall on his request, he went into his room to discuss with his wife. When he finally emerged from his room, his face was rather flushed in exasperation and he simply shook his head in frustration. I took his gestures to indicate that his wife was not in favour of giving me a rebate after all. I left the hall and said to the man stoically, "Never mind, Uncle. Thank you anyway for your kind consideration."

I got along very well with the parents of my 2 private students; in fact, Mrs Chung was the elder sister of Pow Chee, my neighbour at Amoy Lane. This family treated me very well and there were many occasions, like Chinese festivals when I would be invited to have dinner with them, together with the patriarch of the family, Mr Chung Ah Kee, aged about 60 who was one of the leaders of the Chinese Community. Mr Chung Senior, was the president of the Chinese Recreation Club of which I was a member. Table tennis was my forte and I was elected captain, actively engaging other teams in friendly competitions. Mr Chung Senior himself was equally enthusiastic in this game and kindly donated a challenge cup for an open table tennis competition for Taiping residents for the first time. I was tasked to organise the competition. I reached the finals in this inaugural competition defeating my opponents with my strong backhand smashes so much so that the other finalist was smart enough to avoid feeding my back hand. Instead he kept taunting me on my right which was my Achilles heel. My smashes with my right had been terrible and he capitalised on it. Besides he had his bat fixed with some questionable kind of rubber padding, something which I had never seen before which gave the ball plenty of spin whenever he served. As a result, I lost to him eventually in the rubber set and came out runner up.

I got a big jump in my salary when I was appointed Cadet Social Welfare officer while still under probation as a Social Welfare Assistant. I was transferred to the Batang Padang District based in Tapah in 1954 as the District Social Welfare Officer. God had been very merciful to place me in this post when the department created this new post for those who had the Cambridge School Certificate and also knowledge of any of the three vernacular languages among other criterion. To God be the glory.

# Social Welfare Office, Tapah

I was the only staff working here because the case load here was easily manageable although the area I covered was quite large, encompassing the sub-districts of Tanjong Malim and Cameron Highlands in the state of Pahang. I had the use of the office car with a chauffeur. It was very pleasant to work here as there was no work pressure and life here was pretty comfortable. I must point out here that I was given a working space in the Labour Office where both the District Labour Officer, Mr Yeong and his deputy, Mr Lee Chee Weng who was about my age, were very helpful towards me in many ways. For example, when Mr Yeong was told that my landlady coughed almost every morning and night, he voluntarily offered Chee Weng and me a spare room in his quarters free of charge. In return, Chee Weng and I proposed to share his electricity bill which he also declined. So every month, we both would buy a gift for his two little daughters aged 5 and 2 as a token of our appreciation.

Every day, Chee Weng would drive me to the office and for our meals in the town. I made friends with many young teachers and other bachelor officers from other government agencies like Chinese Affairs Department, Public Works Department and police officers whenever we got together for our meals in the coffee shop. Night life was very dull in Tapah, and frequently with some friends, Chee Weng and I would make trips to Kampar in the evenings for relaxation.

Here is one interesting anecdote of my past for your reading. As a result of our evening trips to Kampar with my friends, I befriended a pretty Chinese girl in her late teens by the name of Ah Ching. She helped her parents run an ice kacang and fruit stall which we used to patronise whenever we visited Kampar. Over time and after several rounds of teasing by my friends, I finally dated her one evening. It was a total failure for she brought along her ill-mannered little brother to the cinema. As we walked back to her stall after the show, she did not cross the road with me. Whether this was done on purpose or not, I really did not know. We continued walking on opposite sides of the road. What a ridiculous spectacle! It was as if we had both quarrelled. I was determined that that would be my last date with her.

While working in Taiping, I had gastric pain now and then. It was not very serious then and I was treated with some medication prescribed by the local doctor. Perhaps my pain was due to irregular meals or over indulging on my favourite wanton noodles at a coffee shop for my elevenses almost every alternate day. This discomfort continued even when I was transferred to work in Tapah. Early one morning around 1 o'clock, while everyone was asleep, I suddenly felt the urge to empty my bowels. Fortunately my bedroom came with an attached bathroom. Not only did I purge dark watery stools but I also vomited at the same time so much so that I was getting weak and felt faint. I literally had to crawl on my knees to climb on to my bed. I did not wake Chee Weng for help but he was shocked to see my face so pale in the morning when he woke up. I told him what happened and he quickly took me to the hospital where I was warded for the first time. I was there for a total of six weeks and was diagnosed with a duodenal ulcer after a barium meal test was taken. There was some laceration in the duodenum that caused internal bleeding hence the blackish stool. That was quite an experience which I could not easily forget. I thank God for His healing and saving me from a more severe illness. Upon discharge, I was advised to abstain from spicy and deep fried food.

After a while, I was introduced to a very beautiful young lady, Swee Yeng, four years my junior who was to become my beloved wife. It happened that when I was spending my vacation in Taiping, after an absence of two years, one of the Chung's teenaged daughters cheekily enquired one evening after dinner if I had a girl friend and to which I honestly said, 'no'. This conversation was overheard by their close neighbour, Mrs Chiew, whom I had earlier befriended when I was working in Taiping and she asked if I was really unattached for she wanted to introduce me to her niece, Swee Yeng living in Ipoh. When I confirmed I was unattached, she suggested sending me her photograph and if I was interested to befriend her, she would arrange for us to meet.

Two weeks later, I received a photograph of a beautiful smiling girl. I showed my room mate, Chee Weng, who already had a girl friend in Ipoh, the photo and he was equally impressed by her beauty. He said, "Yip, you must tackle her! I'll give you all my moral support. Quickly reply to set up a meeting with her and I'll drive you to meet her." Of course, I hastened to respond and requested for our meeting on a Saturday evening. I was very happy to receive a very prompt and favourable answer and was invited to Swee Yeng's 8th aunt's house in Farlim, Ipoh. Chee Weng was equally happy too and having driven me to my brother's house in Ipoh that Saturday afternoon, he came again to the house that evening to take me to my rendezvous. "Steady there, old Yip," he whispered to me when we got to our destination. "Don't be nervous but remember to give us a briefing on Monday morning," he teased me cheekily.

As I had not come to know Swee Yeng's 8th aunt and her husband, Mr & Mrs Tan, the Chiews purposely drove all the way from Taiping to Ipoh to set up the introduction. Mrs Chiew is the younger sister of Swee Yeng's 8th aunt. "Ah, here comes the Sor Chai" literally meaning "Silly Boy", announced Mr Chiew when he saw me approaching the door. After seeing me seated comfortably in the front hall, he went inside and in a short while, Swee Yeng emerged all by herself! I was surprised that neither Mr. nor Mrs. Chiew accompanied her for our introduction. "Hello Ah Yeng," I sheepishly greeted her without even extending my hand. "I, Peng Low," I introduced myself and she responded with a gentle nod. We exchanged pleasantries and were soon ushered to the dining hall for a curry chicken dinner prepared by Mrs Tan (the 8th aunt). As dusk set in, the Tans suggested that we all drive to Kampar with the Chiews to pay respects to Swee Yeng's father, Loke Yee Seng who was the eldest brother of Mrs Chiew and Mrs Tan. Mr Loke worked as a teller at the Standard Chartered Bank in Ipoh together with my elder brother. Mr Loke was expecting my visit. In fact, he had mistakenly rushed to the Ipoh Turf Club thinking that I would be brought there by the Tans and Chiews.

It was already past eight when we reached his Sundry Shop in Kampar where I was formally introduced to him, my future father-in-law. Soon we were joined by his younger brother and their very close family friend. As the space was over crowded, the ten of us adjourned to a restaurant for supper. I felt quite out of place here as I was the only outsider sitting at the table. After supper, came this surprise move. Out of the blue, someone suggested we took a stroll. There were only two main roads in Kampar, and Ah Ching's ice kacang stall was located at one of these roads. So it was unavoidable that we strolled past her stall and there she was, serving her customers. I could see her from the corner of my eyes from a distance while walking and chatting with Swee Yeng and her entourage. I could not help but think that Ah Ching saw me too. It had been a very pleasant and enlightening evening for me and before leaving me at my brother's door step, Mr Tan suggested that he would pick me up for breakfast with Swee Yeng the following Sunday morning.

After a hearty breakfast with Swee Yeng and the Tans, we were driven to the market. While Mrs Tan was doing the marketing by herself, Mr Tan had the presence of mind to deliberately excuse himself, leaving the two of us alone in the car. He created the opportunity for us to know each other better. I was not only attracted by her beauty but her soft voice as well. We were very comfortable with each other in our conversation inside the car and I was soon emboldened to ask her if she would like to watch the late night movies. I was so thrilled when she accepted my invitation, so much so, that when a beggar suddenly approached us from nowhere, I happily dug into my pocket and gave him a twenty cent coin. Swee Yeng thought that I was trying to impress her as a generous person which she disclosed to me some time later. In fact, I was advised by my department not to give alms to beggars in order to remove them from the streets and to encourage them to be admitted to our welfare homes.

"Listen everybody, Ah Yeng has made good progress already!" exclaimed Mr Tan to the Chiews when he got home from the market. "They are going to the movies tonight," he added cheerfully much to Swee Yeng's embarrassment.

Meanwhile my elder brother and his fiancée at Pasir Pinji were wondering why I was skipping my dinners with them and they began to suspect that I was dating someone. They had in fact tried to pair me up with his fiancée's younger sister. A week just prior to my acquaintance with Swee Yeng, my brother had discreetly set up a movie date for me with his fiancée's younger sister. My brother told me that we were all going to watch a movie but to my surprise both he and his fiancée abandoned us at the cinema foyer and said they were going to watch another movie instead. They must have been very surprised and disappointed to observe my sudden change in my usual routine. I had begun skipping meals with them and going back to my brother's home rather late at night.

Chee Weng and his boss pestered me for a briefing of my meetings with Swee Yeng. I shared every detail with them and they were happy for me. "You are a fast worker!" exclaimed Chee Weng. "Taking her to the movies so soon after your first encounter?" quipped Mr Yeong.

There was one night after escorting Swee Yeng back to Farlim that I missed the last bus to take me back to my brother's place. It was difficult to get a taxi at that hour too so I walked back hurriedly to Swee Yeng to tell her of my plight. Her uncle was kind enough to drive me to Pasir Pinji at about midnight and ever since that incident, I was invited to spend the night at Farlim. Oh what joy!! Our friendship blossomed to mutual love for each other. Early one evening, Swee Yeng informed me that her father had invited me to stay in his house in Pasir Pinji instead of at Farlim and gratefully I accepted. I had dinner with his family every weekend before we went out for our date.

We had a happy courtship, rid of hiccups and petty squabbles. We had a very wonderful time together every weekend whenever I travelled from Tapah to Ipoh for my dates with Swee Yeng. Courtship was a breeze for both of us as we had mutual respect for each other. Swee Yeng was often teased by her neighbour whenever she went to the hair salon to have her hair nicely done on Saturday mornings. "I'm sure somebody is going on a date tonight," and the good neighbour would wink cheekily at her. We both shared many things in common like watching movies be it in English or Mandarin and having a dislike for Elvis Presley and Andy Lau. We taught each other some popular English and Mandarin love songs. For example, I taught her, "Forever and Ever" and "Till We Meet Again" and in turn Swee Yeng taught me the ever popular Mandarin love song, "Lovers Tears" sung by Poon Sau Kheng. These love songs were chosen as they were so meaningful to us at the time when I was about to leave her because of my transfer from Tapah to Butterworth. We would croon to each other when I left for my further studies in Singapore.

But after some seven months of happy courtship I was given notice of a transfer to the state of Penang and I had to be based in Butterworth on the mainland as a Chinese speaking officer was needed to serve the Chinese population in the northern district of Province Wellesley. We were truly sad to be separated and I had to be contented with seeing my beloved Swee Yeng just about once every month as the journey would take about three hours by taxi between Butterworth and Ipoh compared to a mere forty minutes between Tapah and Ipoh. It was here in Butterworth that I had to purchase a motorbike to perform my duties as there was no vehicle provided by my department. I bought a Velocette motorbike on a government loan. I didn't even know how to ride on it even when I collected it from the shop. I was given oral instructions by the salesman on how to handle the machine. Off I went trusting on my good memory and skills to operate the gear and throttle for acceleration and how to use the brakes. I successfully managed to navigate the busy road back to my home. I even got my motorbike licence without even taking the official test simply because the motor vehicle testers had been using a corner of our office for their theory tests and I had befriended them. I just paid the licence fee!

A year later during our many joyful dates, Swee Yeng casually said to me, "You know, we've been dating each other for quite a while and my grandmother suggested that we should get engaged to stop busybody neighbours from gossiping." Oh was I glad to hear that Swee Yeng was happy to marry me. "Of course, I would be very happy to be engaged to you, "I said without hesitation and assured her that I need not have to consult or get permission from Ku Ma or Sam Ku Cheh. In fact, I had not mentioned to my relatives about my courtship and I was confident that they would accept Swee Yeng into our family.

So Swee Yeng' paternal grandmother who was blind from young and being a devout Buddhist, together with Swee Yeng's aunts, consulted the almanac for an auspicious day for our engagement. They chose a particular day of a lunar month which turned out to be 25th December 1945. It was certainly special for us to become engaged on the day Jesus was born. Here again upon reflection, I can see the wonderful hand of God drawing us close to Him from the days of our youth and I have no doubt that He had blessed us in our relationship as a couple from the early days of our courtship.

We got happily married on 8th September 1956 at the Registry of Civil Marriages, Penang. I was lodging with Sam Ku Cheh as her tenant at Burma Road. She was very kind and generous to give up the comforts of her bedroom for me while she occupied a sleeping space along the corridor just outside the bedrooms upstairs. I only had $1000 in my savings to spend on my wedding and I knew Swee Yeng's father could not depend on any of my relatives for financial help. There was no 10 course wedding dinner but just light refreshment after the signing ceremony at the marriage registry. The registrar reminded me that this was a monogamous marriage and courtship. To my utter surprise, some ten years later, a woman approached me in my office to complain that her husband was not supporting her and having an affair with another woman. She sought help to summon her husband for monthly maintenance. The man turned out to be the registrar himself who officiated my marriage, telling me to be faithful to one wife only and here he was having an extramarital affair!

Together with her father, siblings and relatives, Swee Yeng arrived in Penang a day before the wedding and they stayed in a holiday bungalow by the beach in Tanjung Bungah. Swee Yeng brought along her bridal gown. Her bridal shoes and two pieces of cheongsam for her evening wear arrived only on the eve of our wedding from Hong Kong. Praise God the shoes and cheong sam were of the right fit for she had earlier sent her measurements to her 11th aunt in Hong Kong. How wonderful our Heavenly Father was to send Swee Yeng's trousseau just in time for our wedding! That was indeed a token of His blessing of our wedding for which we are so very grateful.

Another piece of good news came on the eve of our wedding too. I had applied for a government scholarship with my colleague, Ho Yoon Sang some months earlier to study for the Diploma of Social Studies at the University of Malaya in Singapore and we received news that our application for admission was approved. I thought that the government must have rejected my application because it was already September and the academic year was to begin in October. Yoon Sang came to my house that afternoon to enquire whether I had received a telegram because he had just received one in the morning to notify him that he was successful. On learning that I had not received any, he immediately drove me to the telegraph office to enquire. To our joy, I was informed that there was indeed a telegram for me. I quickly tore open the envelope and we were very happy to know that I too, was granted the government scholarship. I was advised to enrol at the university in three weeks' time. Of course, I immediately shared this exciting and happy news with Swee Yeng who had known of my intention to further my studies prior to our marriage. She was happy for me because she understood that it was in the interest of my career to get a professional qualification in social work. Naturally, we both felt sad of the prospect of our impending separation by the end of the month but we comforted each other that I would be home for the vacation at the end of the academic term of ten weeks. I could not help thanking God over and over again for His grace and mercy because I had been applying for this scholarship for the past two years to do this course in Hong Kong but was turned down because of insufficient funds. I am grateful to God for this rejection because the course in Hong Kong was only a certificate in Social Work whereas the one in the University of Malaya was a 2 year post graduate diploma course which was of a higher repute and globally recognised.

Another sacrifice that came with the scholarship was the foregoing of my salary for the two year duration of the course but in lieu of this, Swee Yeng as my dependent would be given a monthly allowance which was adequate. My scholarship covered my tuition, accommodation and travel expenses for my journey to and from the university and also return trips to my home during my term vacations.

As I was making arrangements for my enrolment at the University, I was totally broke for I had exhausted all my savings on my wedding in spite of my frugality. I did not have the money to repay the government for the balance of my outstanding motorcycle loan because I would be on no-pay leave when I entered the university. Although I sold my vehicle, the proceeds were still insufficient to settle the loan. I was surely in financial dire straits not only just to raise the money to settle the loan, but also I did not have the cash for my miscellaneous expenses in Singapore while waiting for the scholarship money to arrive.

By this time, Swee Yeng and I had moved to stay with her father in Ipoh just a week before my departure to Singapore. Swee Yeng was aware of my predicament and she promptly suggested borrowing money from her father to resolve the matter. I agreed but who was to approach the father, for we both felt embarrassed. Like little children, we quickly resorted to a game of scissors, paper and stone and the loser would have to approach the elderly man. I won the first round but Swee Yeng won the second. The third round would be the deciding factor. I survived the final round, so the task of borrowing fell on poor Swee Yeng. We both had a jolly laugh at the outcome and I felt it would indeed be easier for her to approach her father who very willingly lent me a few hundred dollars on being told of my financial plight.

So by late September, I left my wife to stay with her father in Ipoh while I proceeded to Singapore to begin my two year post graduate studies at the University of Malaya as a mature student. In lieu of a basic degree as a pre-requisite, we had to pass the University Entrance Qualifying Exam and a stringent interview as well. My class comprised 12 Malayan and 10 Singaporean social welfare and probation officers of which one student from Singapore had a Bachelor of Arts degree. All the Malayan officers were accommodated at the Dunearn Road Hostel and I had an Indian colleague, Apoo Rahman aged 45 as my room mate. In spite of his age, and married with six children, he was a very diligent student from whom I drew much of my inspiration. He was much disciplined, never late in his attendance and submission of assignments and an avid reader as well. We also had to take compulsory core subjects like principles of social work, social legislation, psychology, sociology and supplementary units like social geography, social history, ethics and social medicine. We had to submit a thesis of no less than 15,000 words. I had very good company when I joined a small group comprising three Malayan and three Singaporean students in studying and sharing our course work. Among the six of us, a Singaporean, Lee Beng Guan, a probation officer was most outstanding. He was married, very intelligent, unassuming and altruistic. He contributed a great deal towards our frequent group meetings which I greatly benefited. We became very close friends throughout the two years at the university. When I was in Ipoh, he even called from Singapore to convey to me the moment the final results were known and later invited my wife and me to his home for dinner just after the convocation at Kallang Theatre. Life at the Bukit Timah campus was really fun and exciting and I made many friends with those taking other courses. I especially enjoyed playing table tennis with some of my college mates. Here I wish to mention three very close friends, in fact, my fellow housemates namely Yahaya, Aman and Mohammad Ghouse who were all reading Economics. They were younger to me and had enrolled in the university a year ahead of me after their secondary education. Little did I realise that I would catch up with them when I was about to retire in Kuala Lumpur and rekindle our friendship. Yahaya joined the elite Malayan Civil Service upon graduation and in due course because of his distinguished career he was bestowed the title 'Dato' which was equivalent to a knighthood. It was my good fortune, that he was the Secretary General of my ministry when I was posted to headquarters as the Deputy Directory of Reformatory Services just prior to my retirement. Aman was there too as the Deputy Secretary General and I felt very comfortable working under them. I was also fortunate to have as my immediate boss, Malcolm Coelho who was my senior fellow course mate at the university. I am very grateful to God for placing me to work under them and much to my benefit He has surely made His move at His precise time.

My other housemate, Mohammad Ghouse in later years was the Chairman of Malayan Tobacco Company in Kuala Lumpur. Although applications for his company's scholarships to study in Cambridge had already been closed, yet he was gracious enough to ask my youngest child, Ming Fai, then aged 19, to submit his application personally to him when he knew of my son's ambition to study engineering in Cambridge. He was impressed with Ming Fai's A level results - A grades in Mathematics, Physics, Biology and Chemistry. Ming Fai was short listed for the interview. I was shocked to hear from Ghouse of his disappointment that Ming Fai, during the interview mentioned that he was not keen to study Engineering but opted for Accounting instead which Cambridge did not offer. Consequently, Ming Fai was unsuccessful in his application, much to our disappointment.

It was during my final year of studies at the university that Swee Yeng gave birth to our first child, Sook Cheng in the District Hospital, Ipoh on 21st April 1958. I was in the midst of my two month practical field work when I received the good news by telephone. I had to delay my leave to return to Ipoh immediately to see my daughter as it would mean that I had to lengthen my field work assignment for that period of leave if I decide to take it. Besides the field work assignment was about to end very soon and that would bring me to the end of my full diploma course. Swee Yeng and her family fully understood my plan. I arrived home eventually by train at about two o'clock in the morning. Swee Yeng's father switched on all the lights in the hall and our room as well as I excitedly touched and kissed Sook Cheng sleeping in her cradle for the first time. I apologised to Swee Yeng for my inability to be near her as she gave me an insight of her delivery which I thanked God for His mercy for keeping both mother and child safe and for His precious gift of a lovely little girl for us. In 1961 we were again blessed with another daughter, Sook Leng and our son, Ming Fai was born in 1964.

# My Career as a Professional Social Worker

After graduating with the Diploma in Social Science in 1958, I was immediately posted to work in Penang, my home town. I was designated Social Welfare Officer for Head Office working as Deputy to the State Social Welfare Officer in charge of the State of Penang. My official duties as a Social Welfare Officer included supervising seven social welfare assistants in their handling of cases pertaining to public assistance to the needy widows, and those seeking admission to homes for children and the elderly. Among the seven social welfare assistants were my two mentors whom I was assigned to understudy all aspects of social work. I was also assigned as Training Officer to other cadet social welfare officers in the State, the marketing officer for the sale of handicrafts like rattan and bamboo baskets made by the physically disabled and as dispute arbitrator trying to reconcile spouses with matrimonial problems. As a professional social worker I was to monitor the progress of voluntary welfare organisations and I was also authorised to grant separation orders between irreconcilable spouses of customary marriages.

Here is one very tragic case of a family dispute which I personally dealt with. One day, a pretty Chinese woman in her late twenties was ushered to my office when she told one of my staff outside that she particularly would like to see a Mr Yap (Hokkien people usually address me as Yap while the Cantonese speaking dialect would call me Yip). It was a strange coincidence that her maiden name was Yap. Her complaint was her husband, a textile salesman who had not been regularly supporting her and her twin daughters. He had been spending his salary on gambling and that led to frequent quarrels.

Now she had sought my help to 'summon' her husband to my office to get from him a regular monthly maintenance. Initially, I had to make her realise that my office was not empowered to 'summon' her husband but to request for his attendance only if he was willing. In addition, I told her that I was not empowered to issue a maintenance order in her favour but merely to negotiate and persuade him to support her and her children. The proper avenue for her redress was the court. Having corrected her notion of my limited authority she still opted my office rather than the court for which I believe she might not have the financial resources to engage a lawyer. So I directed her to file her statement of complaint after which I would invite her husband to my office to seek his views. Subsequently, I sent a memo to her husband for his attendance in order to hear his side of the story. After two weeks had passed, Ms Yap appeared and being told that her husband had not responded to my invitation, she requested that I sent him a reminder to be present at my office a week later. I complied immediately but to my utter shock one late morning before the appointed date an elderly woman was ushered into my room sobbing uncontrollably. She managed to say, "I am Ms Yap's mother. My daughter saw you a couple of weeks ago for maintenance from her husband. Do you remember?" I nodded. "She is dead now" she continued sobbing. "Her husband stabbed her to death early this morning in their bedroom in the presence of the twin daughters. He has been arrested by the police. No wonder I saw him sharpening the knife in the kitchen the night before the murder." I felt very sorry for the old lady, especially the two little seven year old daughters as I listened to her woes. Soon the man was charged in the High Court for murder. I was called as a witness for the prosecution at the trial. That was my first time giving evidence in the witness box before a judge whom I had to address as "My Lord" and I had to swear before him that the evidence I gave shall be 'the truth, the whole truth and nothing but the truth.' I was shown a copy of the deceased woman whom I identified as the one who had filed a complaint for maintenance from the accused. But it was not a pleasant photo because her chest had been cut open for a post mortem to ascertain the cause of her death and stitched back with some coarse strings. I was also directed to produce her statement as proof of her complaint. That was my role as a witness. At the end of the trial, her husband was found guilty of murder and sentenced to death by hanging. He appealed and while waiting for the outcome of the appeal, the prisoner requested repeatedly to see his twin daughters through his lawyer. The grandmother of the girls eventually agreed but on the condition that I was to accompany the twin girls during the visit in place of her. So I escorted the little girls to see their father in the prison. They were very scared when their father was eventually escorted into the special visitors' room for condemned prisoners and they clung to me. After some coaxing and gentle persuasion as well as assurance from me that their father would not hurt them, they slowly inched closer to the outstretched arms of their father who cried unashamedly as he hugged them. But the little girls showed very little or no emotion and still appeared frightened of him. That was my last involvement of the case. Later on, I came to know from the newspapers that his appeal was denied by the Court of Appeal. He appealed again, this time to the Governor for clemency and was lucky to have his death sentence reduced to life imprisonment.

I worked as the Deputy State Welfare Officer for Penang until 1971 when I was promoted to Social Welfare officer Grade 1. I was transferred to a new institution located in Bukit Mertajam, Province Wellesley to work as Superintendent. The institution was a home for the chronically ill patients of various ages and both genders. They were transferred from different public hospitals. These were patients who suffered various forms of incurable illnesses like cancer and tuberculosis which required protracted long term medication and they also had been abandoned by their families. Having such patients in the public hospitals for such a long period would deprive other acute patients of hospital beds. This was an entirely new task for me; looking after terminally ill patients who were transferred by ambulances to my institution from all parts of Malaysia as far south as the state of Johore. As these patients needed continued medication, my ministry had the support of the ministry of Health to second a medical officer from the District Hospital in Bukit Mertajam located just about five kilometres away and a team of 15 nursing staff led by a matron from Penang General Hospital. All of them were provided accommodation within the institution. The resident doctor and I were allotted brand new spacious bungalows within the premises, each just a stone's throw from my office. I was in charge of the whole administration and the general welfare of the patients while the medical team provided medical treatment. We also had a pharmacy as well, equipped with medicine and a van which could be used as an ambulance to send critically ill patients to the hospital. There was also a mortuary. Thus my institution was something like a hospital only that we catered for just the terminally ill patients referred by hospitals. In less than four months, my institution was full to capacity with two hundred patients in all the eight wards.

I felt very sorry for these patients; sickly and without relative or loved ones to care for them. One patient stoically said to me, "I come here with my eyes wide open but when I leave here, my eyes will be closed." I was saddened by his remark. He then gave me a suggestion "How about giving some of the more ambulant patients a picnic by the seaside once in a while?" I was sure that none of the patients had enjoyed this privilege before. This required careful planning. As my van could only take twelve patients I would require additional transport to ferry about thirty patients altogether. The doctor had concurred with my idea and also stressed that the patients had to be accompanied by the nurses and attendants for the duration of the picnic. Finally, I managed to get the services of St John's ambulance and Red Cross to lend me their vehicles. The cooks packed nasi lemak lunch for the whole lot of them. The nurses had the initiative to bring along their transistor radios to provide music and entertained the patients with their dances and singing. The patients enjoyed the breeze by the sea and dipped their feet in the shallow waters with sheer delight like little children as I was briefed later on their return in the early evening.

While on this job I felt great pity for the many helpless bed ridden invalids who needed nursing care. I could feel their misery and some of them had no desire to live. I felt led by God to counsel these folks so as to help them cope with their loneliness and sufferings. My interaction with some of them, both ambulant and bedridden, was richly rewarded. One day, an old Chinese lady held my hand to thank me profusely for having an official to talk to and also for my enquiry about her well being. She said smilingly with just a couple of teeth in her mouth, "You are a very nice man to come to chit chat with us. We never had such kind conversations all these years while we were in the hospitals. No one to talk to us like you did. May God of Heaven bless you richly generation after generation." I was really touched by her sentiments and I thanked her in return. Till this day, I still remember her words and her name was Ong Boey. I understand that the conservative Chinese believe that it is good for young people to be interceded by the elderly with blessings, so I treasure her words inside my heart.

Another interesting episode of my work here had to do with an aged Indian blind patient who used to be a fortune teller. He was often consulted by the visitors of his ward to tell them their fortunes. I did not have the heart to stop his 'hobby' so he could spend his time profitably as he socialised with his patrons and earn some pocket money.

One morning to my surprise he was escorted by an attendant to my office. After seating himself comfortably opposite me, he dismissed the attendant. As he unfurled the top of his sarong, he produced a set of Parker Gold Pens. "Sir, this is for you," he said in Malay. I was totally surprised and asked him the reason. He said, "You have been so good to me and my fellow patients. You never stopped me in my fortune telling in the ward. One day, a patron of mine struck a small lottery and he rewarded me. So I want to give this to you this as an appreciation of your kindness." I had to reject his gift of goodwill politely as not to offend him because as a public servant I was forbidden to accept such gifts which might be misconstrued as bribes. No matter how hard I tried to convince him repeatedly that it was an offence for me to accept the gift, he still persisted. When I stood my ground, he said in exasperation, "If you don't' accept it, you will bring shame to me and I will cut my throat and commit suicide." He was getting emotional. To pacify him, I said, "Thank you. I'll keep it as a remembrance of you." After he left my office, I immediately called the Indian Doctor, Dr Narayanan, to relate to him this episode as I wanted him to explain to the blind man that I would be committing an offence out of his goodwill gesture. Dr Narayanan had earlier gone to the district hospital to attend to other patients some five kilometres away. He agreed to talk to the blind man when he got home for lunch afterwards. The three of us went over the whole issue again but still Dr Narayanan failed to coax him to change his mind. What an adamant fellow. But fortunately, there is a provision in our rules that I could report the matter to my Head of Department in Kuala Lumpur, who will in turn, hand over the gift to the government treasury for disposal. That I did without notifying the blind patient.

Now there is another funny anecdote that will certainly tickle you. One day, I received a surprise phone call from the district hospital to go to their morgue to identify a corpse. "Mr Yip, said the voice, "Do you remember some time last week you sent a patient by the name of Marimuthu to my hospital? Well, he has just passed away yesterday and we put him in the mortuary. Unfortunately, there was also another Indian corpse sharing the same morgue whose name is also Marimuthu and he did not have any relative. My attendants who put them inside the mortuary can't tell for sure which one belongs to your centre. So I hope you can come and take away yours, after you've identified the bodies." Immediately, I responded as I had some vague memory of Marimuthu's face. I should have brought along one of my nurses or attendants who had attended to Marimuthu with me for this identification exercise. I was ushered into the morgue, the stench of which was very nauseating and I saw the two corpses with the name Marimuthu placed side by side. They were about the same age and build and appeared to look alike. No wonder their staff could not differentiate the two. I too was stumped! I regretted not bringing my staff along. So I trusted my gut instinct and simply pointed to one of the two to be sent back to my centre for burial. To my surprise and relief I chose the correct one. My staff could easily identify him as they prepared the body for burial.

By 1974, there was a growing number of young drug addicts in the country and the government felt there was a need to rehabilitate them and so space had to be provided for them. Our ministry was tasked to provide treatment and rehabilitation for them. This social problem was quite serious. Two of my wards inside my centre had to be emptied in order to admit and treat the drug addicts. Thus many of my chronically ill patients had to be transferred to ordinary old folks' homes in Alor Setar and Taiping. That was the start of my role as a Counsellor and Head of the first Drug Rehabilitation Centre of my ministry in Bukit Mertajam.

Initially, all the twenty five drug dependents admitted to my centre for twelve months of rehabilitation were voluntary cases and not committed by drug order. While the medical staff attended to their medical needs like detoxification especially during their drug withdrawal period, the counselling was provided by myself with the help of an unqualified senior social welfare assistant. Also the spiritual needs of the Muslim residents were attended to by an imam (a Muslim religious teacher) while my matron, a Christian would share Christian teachings with a couple of the Christian inmates.

There was one traumatic experience with these drug addicts which I wish to record here. One evening, I had given permission to the inmates to watch the live telecast of the Thomas Cup badminton match between Malaysia and Indonesia, even though it was past bed time. While the match was in progress I decided to get up from my chair for a stretch at around 11 p.m. I caught the sight of smoke coming out from the centre. I was surprised that I was not alerted by any of my staff. Quickly, I walked into the centre and to my horror, I saw a burning mattress in the open ground just outside the wards of the residents. A small group of the residents quickly scampered away as I approached them and in their hurried getaway, left behind a bench on which were traces of burnt match sticks, cigarette ends and a couple of teaspoons which were telling evidence that they had been smoking drugs on the sly, in spite of our attempts to make the centre drug free. The inmates must have taken advantage of our manpower shortage at that particular time. An emergency roll call was sounded and the resident medical officer was quick to come to my assistance. I told him of the problem and he agreed to search the inmates for drugs and at the same time take their urine samples for drug analysis – all twenty five of them. A couple of nurses and attendants were roped in for this exercise. To our surprise, we found two straws of drugs concealed inside the underwear of two inmates when they were told to strip! I was very angry with these two who had voluntarily applied admission to the rehabilitation centre and without having to pay fees in the first place. I immediately called the police to arrest them for the offence of possession of illicit drugs, and to prevent them from sharing the drugs with the others. It took us a long time to take all the twenty five urine samples, and as the time dragged on, one of the inmates, an ex-postman had the gall to ask to be given supper. I angrily asked him in the presence of the whole gathering who and what provoked me in the first place to conduct this wretched exercise at that unearthly hour and abandoning the luxury of watching the Thomas Cup match. I reasoned with them by saying, "All of you came here on your own volition to seek rehabilitation at the full expense of the government and we welcomed you. You had signed a contract to abide by our rules and regulations. You are in a way, our guests but tonight some of you have been caught doing the things you are not supposed to do. I am very disappointed with all of you. And you have the cheek to ask for supper. Who do you think you are?" I pointed at the ex-postman. There was complete silence as they listened to my tirade.

Both the two inmates with the possession of drugs were subsequently sentenced to six months of imprisonment. One of them requested that I should not inform his parents of his predicament but I told him that it was my duty to notify them of his present circumstances. He said tearfully, "This is the first time that I'm going to prison. My parents will be very hurt." I responded, "I'm glad that you've some feelings for your parents, so the more you should not disappoint them. Remember it's your duty to support them in their old age in return for bringing you up. How do you propose to fulfil your moral obligation? Think about it." He burst out crying to his parents. "I deserve this punishment. I've been very aggressive. I'll turn over a new leaf when I come out of jail." He assured his parents as they listened to him with teary eyes.

During the course of my thirty one year career in the Ministry of Welfare Services, I had served as Superintendent in three drug rehabilitation centres located in Bukit Mertajam in the state of Penang with twenty five inmates, Kuala Kubu Bahru in the state of Selangor with one hundred and fifty inmates and finally Kampung Raja in the state of Terengganu. By then, I was in my early fifties. When I was working at Kuala Kubu Bahru and Kampung Raja, Swee Yeng and I made the decision to allow the children to remain in Penang for their education. Sook Cheng, by then was already having a successful career as a piano teacher and when I was at Kampung Raja, Sook Leng was already studying in Perth, Western Australia while Ming Fai was granted an Asean scholarship to study his A levels at Hwa Chong High School in Singapore. Swee Yeng remained by my side to keep me company. There is one episode in the Kampung Raja centre that warrants special mention in my chronicles. Admissions to this and other drug rehabilitation centres by this time were for those under court orders to spend a period of two years of rehabilitation. Many of these who were admitted were not only drug users, but the majority had criminal records too such as causing grievous hurt, armed robbery, gang fights and so on. Controlling them had always been a problem as we did not have cells to lock them up when they have finished their chores or exercises. They all slept in crammed, overcrowded open dormitories. Ragging and bullying by the senior inmates on the freshies was rampant but discreetly done with their own 'sentries'. The victims were simply too scared to report to us of their victimisation and our human resources were not only limited in number but also in training, with a number of them being females.

So it was my misfortune that I was awakened one early morning in my quarters to be notified that an Indian inmate who had just been admitted to the centre a day before was found dead in his bed when he failed to attend the early morning roll call. I had the fright of my life when I saw a dead body neatly covered with a blanket. I concluded that he must have been the victim of excessive ragging during the night. While the police report was being filed, I took steps to station some of my staff around the high fences to forestall the perpetrators from escaping and at the same time to secure all exit points around the centres. The police soon rounded up six senior leaders among the addicts as suspects after interviewing me and some of my staff and the body was sent to the hospital for post-mortem. The cause of death was asphyxia according to the medical report.

Not only had I to report to my headquarters of this incident but I also had the onerous duty to notify the parents of the deceased. I was also hounded by reporters the following day for more details but I politely informed them that the rules forbade me from communicating with the media and I advised them to approach the officers in my headquarters for the news they sought. You can imagine the trauma I was experiencing. The parents of the deceased who lived in Kuala Lumpur were very angry with me and hinted they would sue me as the Head of the institution and also my ministry for failing to protect their son and provide him rehabilitation as ordered by the court. My minister was furious when the incident was reported to her and ordered the Director-General of the ministry to personally conduct an investigation immediately.

The next morning, the Director-General sent the Head of the Drug Rehabilitation Services, Mr Lee who is a fellow Christian to conduct the enquiry, paying particular attention among other factors as to whether I was present in my quarters on the night of this incident as required by our rules. This I came to know later from a very close friend of mine in the HQ.

On the same night, the brother of the deceased and three of his friends arrived from Kuala Lumpur to collect the body. As there was only one small hotel in this village and all the rooms had been taken up, they had no place to sleep for the night. When they approached me with this problem, I offered them a room in my quarters and the use of a telephone which they accepted. When I suggested to my wife in Cantonese to prepare milo drinks for the guests, one of them answered in perfect Cantonese that they had just had supper and declined the drinks, much to my surprise. The next morning, I assisted them to get the body released expeditiously from the hospital after the autopsy was done and soon they were on their way home. Meanwhile the six suspects were subsequently charged for murder.

Another equally frightening incident occurred in the centre while Mr Lee was having some discussion with me and my staff. It was raining cats and dogs when suddenly an attendant rushed in shouting, "Sir, the inmates are fighting at the quadrangle with one another using weapons from the workshop!" Immediately I ordered a staff to ring the police while I rushed out to the quadrangle followed by two very loyal and dedicated staff, a Chinese Counsellor and a Malay driver. There in the heavy downpour, the Chinese inmates armed with sharp weapons like screw drivers, chisels and hammers were confronting the Malay inmates who were flinging broken pieces of glass from window panes and fluorescent tubes at the Chinese. I snatched the weapons from the Chinese who surrendered without much resistance for they had some respect for me and they were quickly bundled by my driver who was by my side during this time. I believe God must have been shielding me from the pieces of broken glass thrown by the Malays at the Chinese - some of whom received cuts. Soon the police arrived wearing their special 'riot gear' and calm was restored after a couple of leaders from both sides were picked up by the police. Still, we had to segregate the two races and to re-arrange their sleeping accommodation for obvious reasons. It was an ordeal for me – first, the murder and two nights later, the racial riot.

As a result of these two unfortunate incidents I soon found myself drawing closer to God praying fervently for His guidance and mercy just before going to bed every night to face the challenging days ahead, not knowing what the outcome of these two incidents would be. I knew I could trust God as I laid all my worries on Him in my prayers. Each time I received the subpoena to appear in court as a witness at the murder trial of the six accused I would pray fervently every night for His mercy and wisdom to guide me in my testimony on the witness stand and to shield me from embarrassment when answering the questions posed to me by their defence counsel. I had been subpoenaed three times to attend the court hearing but each time it was postponed for some reason or other. On the fourth subpoena, I saw the six accused in court for the first time and I expected there would be a hearing and finally I would be put on the witness stand to face their counsel. I prayed silently to God for His wisdom and tender mercies. Suddenly, a court official came up to me to say the judge would like to see me in his chambers. I wondered with some trepidation what the reason was as I was ushered in. The judge said to me, "The charge of murder has been reduced to a lesser offence of manslaughter by the prosecution and all six of them will plead guilty as advised by their counsel. So your attendance is not required." I sighed with relief. "You have truly answered my prayers, O God."

I was totally exonerated from any blame for these two traumatic events by my ministry and after the dust had settled, I was transferred to fill up the post of Deputy Director for Reformatory Services in the HQ, drawing the same salary as my previous position at the Drug Rehabilitation Centre. A couple of years later, as the result of a total revision of our salary structure, my post of Deputy Director was upgraded from Super scale J to G, a salary increase of a couple of hundred ringgit which I enjoyed until my retirement the following year in 1983.

Such unexpected blessings from the Lord!

# My Testimonies of God's Divine Power

I want to testify that God can do anything and everything for He has promised us in **Luke 1:37 – "For with God nothing will be impossible."** I shared this extraordinary testimony with members of my church assembly in Singapore.

Some time in late 1982, a year just before my retirement, I suddenly had the compulsion to pay a visit to the parents of the Indian drug addict who was killed in my centre. I wanted to offer my humble apologies to the bereaved parents in person for my failure to protect their son, although I had offered my condolences and apologies to them by phone from the drug centre initially. I was stationed in Kuala Lumpur and I remembered the family was staying in the Telecom quarters in Brickfields. I strongly felt that it would be proper and ethical for me to pay a courtesy call to them even though it was belated. Although I encouraged myself to do it, I had some reservations because I was unable to recall the name of the deceased nor the names of his parents and their address. I only remembered that his father worked in the Telecom department and lived in the Telecom quarters in Brickfields and was a member of the Malaysian Indian Congress, a political party. It was like looking for the proverbial needle in the haystack. I felt discouraged and was wondering whether I should abort my attempt to visit. How would the couple react to my presence if I indeed caught up with them? Would I not be reviving their pain and grief? Would they be angry with me and accuse me of failing in my duty and why only meet them in person at this point in time? These thoughts seemed to discourage me from implementing my plan. I began to have cold feet after all and thus buried my anxiety to visit the couple for a while. But the desire cropped up from time to time for a period of weeks and then months. My retirement was drawing closer and soon I would be returning to Penang for good. If I were to abort my plan totally I would never have the chance to meet the couple to express my apologies and condolences in person. In the end, I convinced myself to go and search for this couple even if they might be furious with me. I put my faith in God to guide me there and to accomplish my mission.

So one Sunday afternoon after lunch, I drove alone on the roads of Brickfields looking left and right for any indication of the Telecom quarters. After a while I spotted a signboard with bold lettering "Telecom Quarters Brickfields" and I was just about to pass by the entrance leading to the row of buildings that housed the staff quarters. Immediately, I stepped on the car brakes without signalling to the cars that were behind me as I was so thrilled in finally tracing the quarters after so much uncertainty in the past months. The moment my car stopped there was a loud honk and the screech of brakes just behind me and I thought that an accident was about to occur. I got out of my car quickly to assess if there was any damage to the cars when I was confronted by an angry bespectacled Indian man who gestured to express his annoyance at me. I could not blame him and quickly apologised to him. Thank God our cars did not collide and our car bumpers were just only a whisker away from each other. I apologised to him profusely and explained that I was not properly focused on the road. I told him who I was trying to locate and that I had no idea the names of this couple. I was so sorry for the loss of their son. I only had a scant knowledge of where the father worked and that his other son worked as an Engineer for ESSO. "I wonder if you know this family." I said sheepishly. To my utter amazement, this stranger answered, "I am that father". This reminded me of the Samaritan woman talking to Jesus at Jacob's well not knowing that He was the Messiah she was looking for. What a surprise to both of us and meeting in such a manner on the verge of a motor collision! I was relieved to see he was smiling at me and not angry. "Oh, thank you Heavenly Father for bringing us together this very hour. How kind of you Father to draw us together on this road to meet each other at the same time. Surely you have planned this for us. Indeed, you can do anything and everything for those who believe in you and your timing is so perfect", I quietly said to myself. I wondered if we would have met if I had decided to venture earlier or postponed it to some other time.

"Come follow me and I'll take you to my house," he offered. He then introduced me to his wife and invited me to have lunch with them. I told him the purpose of my calling on them. I offered them my humble apologies and condolences all over again but in person this time. They both understood my sincere good intentions and nodded their heads in approval as they shared their food with me. While enjoying our meal, their son, the engineer came home and immediately recognised me and warmly welcomed me. He too, joined us for lunch.

Another promise from the Lord which I hold very dear is **"And whatever things you ask in prayer, believing, you will receive." - Matthew 21: 22**

Having graduated with a Bachelor of Accountancy degree from the National University of Singapore, and while in the second year of his articles for the professional qualifications of Certified Public Accountant at Price Waterhouse, Ming Fai, my son, was by then in his early twenties. He applied and was admitted to read Law as an affiliated student at Wolfson College, Cambridge. Since he already had a first degree, he was permitted to do his Law Degree in two years instead of three.

But unfortunately, he failed to obtain a full scholarship and was awarded a bursary of a thousand pounds annually. Ming Fai was rather hesitant to proceed to Cambridge at that time for I only had enough funds for just one year of his two year studies. I was prepared to mortgage our house to the bank for a study loan so that he could fulfil his dream and not miss this golden opportunity. I persuaded him to proceed for there is a Chinese saying which I believe goes like this – "when the boat begins to dock at the wharf, it automatically straightens itself as it berths." At that point in time, I was already re-employed on a part-time basis during my twilight years as a field-work supervisor to undergraduate students doing their degree in Social Development and Administration (SDA) at the University Science Malaysia, in Penang. The academic year was drawing to a close and there was a proposal by the School of SDA to upgrade the two of the three part-time posts to full time supervisors in the coming year. That was indeed good news for me and I could comfortably finance Ming Fai's education in Cambridge if only I was appointed full-time which came with a four figure salary. Naturally, my wife and I sought the Lord in prayer fervently and steadfastly for the success of my application. We were reminded in Philippians 4:6-7 "Be anxious for nothing but in everything by prayer and supplication with thanksgiving, let your requests be made known to God; and the peace of God which surpasses all understanding will guard your hearts and minds through Christ Jesus." Truly my God of miracles answered my humble petitions. While Ming Fai just started his studies at Cambridge, I was given a yearly tenure and the contract was subject to renewal by the School of SDA. Still I was very contented with the appointment and at the end of the academic year, God was compassionate enough to have my contract renewed the following year. Therefore, together with my monthly pension as a government retiree and my salary from the University, my financial worries were happily resolved as I encouraged Ming Fai to focus on his studies while I worked to support him. After the renewal of my contract the following year, the School had enough funds to employ only one full-time supervisor and I willingly stepped down to take the part-time post to enable a young fellow supervisor to continue working on a full-time basis. By then, Ming Fai had already completed his studies and was ready for his convocation. Thank God for His perfect timing.

Not only did my son benefit from our Heavenly Father's benevolence, we also had some savings to enable us to attend Ming Fai's convocation as well as to enjoy a brief tour of Scotland prior to the convocation. Does this not remind us in Matthew 15:32-38 of Jesus feeding the crowd of four thousand people with seven loaves of bread and some fish and after the crowd had eaten, His disciples were able to gather up seven large baskets full of fragments from the left over?

God by His tender mercies continued to shower wisdom and blessing on Ming Fai and he passed with Second Class Honours (Upper) for his Law degree, in spite of falling ill while sitting for one paper and continuing the examination in the sick bay. The President of Wolfson, Sir David William who was also the Vice-Chancellor of Cambridge University was conferred a knighthood by the Queen. He set up the Sir David William prize for the top law student to commemorate the bestowal of his knighthood. He then announced "......and the inaugural winner of the Sir David William prize goes to a foreign student, Yip Ming Fai." Imagine our shock and surprise as fellow graduands and guests and faculty staff cheerfully applauded Ming Fai as he approached the rostrum to receive the award. When he returned to his seat, I whispered to Ming Fai, "Why didn't you sound us earlier on? You surprised me." And he smilingly answered, "I only knew it now!" Oh, as parents, we were so proud of his achievement and as he sat down I told him how proud I was of him. A charming English lady sitting next to me overheard our conversation and congratulated us warmly saying, "Must have been a wonderful surprise to all of you."

Not only did Ming Fai do well in Cambridge he also through God's guidance, secured a first class honours in the Law Society

Final for solicitors of England and Wales. For his success, he was richly rewarded with five hundred pounds by the Law firm which sponsored his professional studies and pupilage as a solicitor.

Blessed are those who show obedience to God. There are many passages in the Bible that constantly exhort the believer to obey God. "If you diligently obey the voice of the Lord your God, to observe carefully all His commandments which I command you today, that the Lord our God will set you high above all nations of the earth." **Deuteronomy 28:1**.

Another incident during which I really felt the hand of God and His omnipotence was when I travelled to America to study the treatment and rehabilitation of drug dependent users. This was around the time when I was transferred to Bukit Mertajam in 1972 when the government was about to introduce the first drug rehabilitation program in the centre.

I chanced to sit next to a Chinese couple around my age when I took the connecting flight from Hong Kong to the States. After exchanging pleasantries with one another, we became acquainted and I got to know Mr Cheong and learnt that he worked in a bank in New York. I told him of my professional development course in New York, and my flight itinerary which included transits at Los Angeles and San Francisco. Mr. Cheong told me that there was a direct flight from Los Angeles to New York and he casually asked me if I had a day engagement in San Francisco to which I said 'no'. Mr Cheong said, "My wife and I are taking the connecting flight from Los Angeles to New York. If you like, I can help you re-schedule your flight at the airport in Los Angeles and we can all fly to New York together. I am familiar with the Hotel Plaza in New York where you will be staying. We would like to welcome you as our guest in our home and I'll drive you to the hotel the next morning." What a generous offer and kind gesture from a total stranger!

I can truly see God's Hand in allocating my seat next to Mr Cheong. After getting my ticket re-routed in Los Angeles, the Cheongs and I parted company. They were seated in the Business class from then on while I remained in the economy section. Should they have travelled in the Business class from Hong Kong, I would not have met this Good Samaritan. "O Heavenly Father, how great Thou art and I thank Thee for Thy faithfulness."

It was also in America, that I felt once again God's Healing hand upon me. In **John 5:6-9**, Jesus healed a man who was infirmed by the pool at Bethesda. "Rise take up your bed and walk," Jesus told the man and immediately he was made well, took up his bed and walked.

I was walking from Hotel Plaza in New York to the United Nations Building where I was to report to the UN Development Programme Directorate. There I would be briefed regarding my study tour and given my fellowship stipend. I had hardly walked for five minutes when I felt a sudden gripping pain on my right knee. I tried to ignore the pain as I continued my journey but the sensation lingered and became increasingly excruciating. I could barely walk any further nor stand on my right leg. "O God, what is happening to me?" I asked.

"My first day in America and I am being incapacitated." I prayed for God's divine healing. My other concern was not having any medical insurance and I was worried that any medical treatment would be very costly indeed. There were no benches along the pavement so I had no choice but to sit on the kerb to massage my right knee cap. "O how can I make it to the UN building? It's so near and yet so far," I lamented to myself. I knew that God is omniscient. Before long, a black American in full suit squatted beside me and enquired if I was in pain. I told him of this sudden seizure and could not understand how this pain came about. He rolled up my trousers and began to massage the knee cap which appeared to be normal as there were no tell tale signs of any bruising or swelling. We struck up a conversation and I told the stranger the reason for my visit to America. Minutes passed, I could feel the pain slowly waning off as this Good Samaritan continued to massage my leg. He stretched and bent my knee a few times and I did not feel the excruciating pain any more. Upon his encouragement, I was able to stand on the affected leg and walked a few steps without any trouble. I truly believe that my Almighty God sent this angel to lay His healing hand on me. I thanked the stranger profusely and continued my journey to the UN building. I recall in **Jeremiah 33:3** "Call to Me, and I will answer you, and show you great and mighty things, which you do not know." Just as we dial 999 in Malaysia in an emergency, my God's emergency hotline is 333. He answers your earnest prayer for He is the Almighty God and does things which will astonish us.

# Epilogue

SUNDAY, 21 SEPTEMBER 2008. I received a phone call from the doctor shortly after that morning's Sunday service requesting me to go to the hospital without further delay. Right then, I knew my father was slipping away.

During the wake service, we were reminded of Psalm 90:10a *"The days of our lives are seventy years; and if by reason of strength they are eighty years."* We thank God for giving my father the strength to live fully to a ripe old age of eighty. From the many testimonies I heard during the wake and funeral services, both in public and expressed privately, I was delighted to know that he had touched many lives and was fondly remembered by all who knew him well.

Through His grace and mercy, God gave this faithful servant advance notice that He would be bringing him home in a year's time. My father took the news that he had terminal idiopathic pulmonary fibrosis calmly. In his final year, he managed to attend to his personal affairs in his usual meticulous way. With Sook Leng's encouragement, he began writing these memoirs and completed them just in time as his legacy for his children and grandchildren. He even managed to select a niche at All Saints Memorial Chapel (Singapore), for his final resting place and waited patiently for his appointed time.

I was more circumspect when I heard the bad news as I had never experienced death within my immediate family before. I anticipated that as his condition worsened, we might have to make difficult medical decisions for him. On that fateful Friday morning, 19th September 2008, we had to make the first of such difficult choices.

When I first saw my father in the hospital on Friday, he had an oxygen mask and was clearly gasping for air. The doctor asked us if we wanted to put him on a ventilator so that oxygen could be pumped directly into his body. Given his condition, there was a real risk that the doctors might not be able to wean him off the ventilator eventually and he could be dependent on it for a prolonged period. As we could not bear to see him suffer, we readily requested that he be put on the ventilator.

On Saturday morning, we were briefed on the extent of his illness. Aside from his breathing difficulties, he had contracted pneumonia, suffered a heart attack and had internal bleeding. Their immediate concern was to prevent another heart attack from occurring. For that, the doctors asked us if we wanted them to administer a drug which was beneficial for his heart but could worsen the internal bleeding, thereby accelerating his demise. Sook Cheng and I were leaning against this risky treatment. To get some assurance, I even asked the senior consultant that had it been his own father, would he have proceeded with this treatment. He replied that he would not have done so.

Before we firmed up our decision, Sook Cheng suggested that we should consult our father who was still conscious and lucid. Although he could not verbalise his response, he was able to articulate it in writing. His exact words were: "*I WANT TO GO HOME TO BE WITH THE LORD*". We were grieved by his response, but God's peace soon replaced our sorrow. We knew his time was drawing to a close and any subsequent decisions we had to make concerning his well being would be relatively straight forward.

When I arrived at the hospital on Sunday morning, the doctor informed me that my father's blood pressure had slipped to a critical level the previous night and early that morning. They had given him more drugs to bring it back up. I immediately understood that they were merely keeping him alive long enough for us to bid our final farewell. So when the doctor asked us if we wanted him to perform CPR when his heart stopped, we declined as we no longer wanted to delay his final journey home.

At precisely 2.00 pm that afternoon, 21$^{st}$ September, my father passed away peacefully. Mum, Sook Cheng, William, Melissa, Sandie and I, along with our church friends, Edward, Daisy, Steven, Puong Huat and Yvonne were at his bedside when he departed. Sook Leng and Austin could not fly to Singapore on time but they, Aaron and Joelle managed to say their final goodbye to him through the phone.

My father was truly dedicated to his family. He was loving, kind, compassionate and thoughtful, even until the very last moments of his life by sparing us from having to make too many difficult decisions for him. Sook Leng has often reminded me that while we can choose our friends, we can never choose our family. If given a chance to start all over again, my sisters and I, together with our spouses, William, Austin and Sandie, will not want another person to be our father.

*Ming Fai*

Our family would like to thank the following individuals (in no particular order) for their prayers, words of comfort and presence in the hospital, his wake and funeral services:

## Relatives & friends of my father

Ignatius and Cecilia Chiew, Yee Cheong, Yee, Hong, Fong, Tony Tee, Say Yee, Sam Yee, Uncle Peng Ho, Tony Teoh, Sally, Alan, Rosalind, Chin Ho, Cynthia, Chian Beng, William Chua, Tan Sri and Puan Sri Khoo Kay Por

## Bethesda Serangoon Church

Elders, Deacons, Members of Serangoon Care Group, Chinese Bible Class, Family Life Committee, Assembly Evangelistic Committee, Dr. Leong Choon Kit (dad's physician), Ken and Joanne (video presentation), Christmas and Angeline and all other members of this church

## Bukit Panjang Methodist Church

Reverend Poh Heow Lee, Reverend Paul Thian, Billy & Esther, Thomas & Sophia Bay, Kwong Hwa & Mei Har, Thomas & May Ang, Richard & Joanna, Brady & Adeline, Antony & Shirley, Geok Sum & Bonnie, Henry & Wendy, Vincent & Karen, Chris & Helena, Kenny & Josephine, George & Jeff, Yew Wai & Katherine, Dick, Ivy, Callie, Karen Nah, Agnes, Chin Eng, David Seah, Sim Beng Huat, Augustine, Tony, Yue Heng, Charles, Lay Tin

<u>Island Glades Gospel Centre, Penang</u>

Elders, Deacons and church members

<u>Taiping Gospel Hall</u>

Mr. and Mrs. Daniel Jevaraj

and colleagues and other friends of the family.